Cha

Legal
Spelling Checker

Also published by Chambers

Chambers Good Spelling
Chambers Medical Spelling Checker
Spell Well
Type Right!

Nicola Wood is a qualified lawyer and also a freelance
writer and editor.

Chambers

Legal
Spelling Checker

Edited by

Nicola Wood

Published 1990 by W & R Chambers Ltd,
43–45 Annandale Street, Edinburgh EH7 4AZ

British Library Cataloguing in Publication Data

Wood, Nicola
   Chambers legal spelling checker.
   1. Law. Terminology
   I. Title
   340'.014

ISBN 0-550-18042-7

Typeset by Pillans & Wilson Specialist Litho Printers Ltd. Edinburgh
Printed in Singapore by Loi Printing Pte Ltd

Preface

Good spelling is essential for everyone in the legal profession, whether they be solicitor, barrister, advocate or legal secretary. It is rare, though, to find people who can spell all the words they are called upon to type or write during the course of their working day. A general dictionary might not contain specialized legal vocabulary, and although a legal dictionary is useful, it is not always necessary to know the precise *meaning* of a word, but simply its spelling, in order to be able to transcribe acurately and quickly from a dictation or notes.

Chambers Legal Spelling Checker contains over 25000 words clearly arranged in alphabetical order. It combines a wide range of English and Scottish legal terms, covering conveyancing, criminal and civil litigation, statute law, corporate and finance law, law of probate and succession, jurisprudence and other areas of law. It also encompasses Latin and French legal words and phrases as well as a large general vocabulary. It thus avoids the need for two or more different reference sources. Word definitions have not been included, as the primary intention of the book is to facilitate the quick and easy checking of spelling.

Additional sections contain words liable to be confused, some commonly used abbreviations and principal cities and countries of the world.

In all, *Chambers Legal Spelling Checker* is a handy desktop reference.

About this book

The 25000 words are clearly arranged in alphabetical order. In some instances there is more than one correct spelling for a word, and which spelling is used is a matter of individual preference. Alternative spellings are listed in the correct alphabetical position, and therefore the alternative spellings of a single word may not be listed consecutively.

The plurals of most nouns are usually formed simply by adding s to the singular, but noted exceptions are listed.

For verb endings -ize rather than -ise has been used consistently. All trade names have been marked with an ®, as in Ansafone® and Xerox®.

Words which are not spelled the way they sound

Certain words might cause difficulty because they are not spelled the way they sound. In particular note that people pronounce legal Latin in differenct ways. The following is a short list of popular pronunciations which are not the only possibilities.

'e' at the end of a word is sounded 'ay' (day) e.g.

se	(pronounced 'say')
re	(pronounced 'ray')
de	(pronounced 'day')
habile	(pronounced 'habilay')

'i' at the end of a word is sounded 'ee' e.g.

loci	(pronounced 'lowkee')
fori	(pronounced 'foree')
crediti	(pronounced 'creditee')

'c' can be sounded 's', 'k', 'ch' or 'sh' e.g.

centrum	(pronounced 'sentroom')
capias	(pronounced 'kapeeas')
coelo	(pronounced 'chaylo')
facie	(pronounced 'faysheeay')

'g' can be sounded 'g' or 'j' e.g.

grassum	(pronounced 'grassoom')
gestae	(pronounced 'gestaye')
generis	(pronounced 'jenereess')

'j' can be sounded 'j' or 'y' e.g.

jus	(pronounced 'yooss')
judicatum	(pronounced 'yoodikatoom' or 'joodikatoom')
juris	(pronounced 'yooris' or 'jooris')

'au' is sounded 'ow' (iow) e.g.

| causa | (pronounced 'cowsa') |
| auctor | (pronounced 'owktor') |

'u' is sounded 'oo' or 'u' e.g.

uberrimae	(pronounced 'ooberrimay')
suam	(pronounced 'sooam')
umquhile	(pronounced 'oomkwilly')
ultra	(pronounced 'ultra')

'ae' is sounded 'ay' (day) or 'aye' (sky) e.g.

| quaesitum | (pronounced 'kwayseetoom' or 'kwayeseetoom') |
| praepositura | (pronounced 'praypositoora' or 'prayepositoora') |

Two vowels together at a word ending are sounded separately e.g.

caveat	(pronounced 'cav-e-at')
habeas	(pronounced 'haybee-as')
fidei	(pronounced 'fiday-ee')
poenitentiae	(pronounced 'peenitensee-ay')
die	(pronounced 'dee-ay')

Other legal words are pronounced oddly. Again the list is not full, neither are the pronunciations the only ones used.

bête noire	(pronounced 'bet nwar')
caution	(pronounced 'cay-shun')
cy près	(pronounced 'see pray')
roup	(pronounced 'rowp (bough)')
poind	(pronounced 'pind')
feu	(pronounced 'few')
lieu	(pronounced 'loo')
multures	(pronounced 'mooters')
puisne	(pronounced 'puny')
spuilzie, tailzie, assoilzie	(pronounced 'spooly', 'taily', 'assoily')
feme sole (covert)	(pronounced 'fam sole, (covert)')
renvoi	(pronounced 'rahvwa')
pur autre vie	(pronounced 'pure otre vee')

Word division and word breaks

Common sense and the overall appearance of the printed page are important considerations for end-of-line divisions.

If a word has to be split at the end of a line, the split should be between two syllables. The word should be divided according to its sound when speaking aloud so that its meaning is entirely clear to the reader.

A split should not divide a word so that a part of it, which is a word in its own right, is divided e.g. testamentary should be divided testament-ary and not test-amentary, because testament is a word in its own right and amentary is not.

A single letter of a word should not begin or end a line.

Aa

a caelo usque ad centrum
a fortiori
a mensa et thoro
a posteriori
a priori
ab initio
ab intestato
aback
abandon
abandoned
abandoning
abandonment
abase
abased
abasement
abashed
abasing
abate
abated
abatement
abatement notices
abatement of action
abatement of debts
abatement of legacies
abatement of nuisances
abating
abattoir
abbreviate
abbreviated
abbreviating
abbreviation
abdicate
abdicated
abdicating
abdication
abdomen

abdominal
abduct
abduction
abet
abetted
abetting
abeyance
abhor
abhorred
abhorrence
abhorrent
abhorring
abide by
abided by
abiding
abiding by
abilities
ability
abitrator
abject
abjuration
able
ably
abnormal
abnormalities
abnormality
abnormally
aboard
abode
abode by
abolish
abolition
abolitionist
abominable
abominably
abominate
abominated
abominating
abomination
abort
abortion
abortive

abound
about
above
abrasion
abrasive
abrasively
abreast
abridge
abridged
abridgement
abridging
abroad
abrogate
abrupt
abruptness
abscond
absence
absent
absentee
absolute
absolute assignment
absolute decree
absolute discharge
absolute duties
absolute liability
absolute privilege
absolute title
absolutely
absoluteness
absolution
absolve
absolved
absolving
absolvitor
absorb
absorbent
absorption
abstain
abstainer
abstemious
abstention
abstinence

1

Aa

abstract
abstract title
abstruse
abstrusely
absurd
absurdities
absurdity
abundance
abundant
abuse
abuse of process
abused
abusing
abusive
abusively
abysmal
abysmally
academic
academically
academies
academy
ACAS
accede
acceded
acceding
accelerate
accelerated
accelerating
acceleration
accelerator
accent
accentuate
accentuated
accentuating
accept
acceptable
acceptance
acceptilation
acceptor
access
accessibility
accessible

accessibly
accession
accessories
accessory
accessory action
accessory obligation
accident
accidental
accidentally
acclaim
acclamation
acclimatization
acclimatize
acclimatized
acclimatizing
accommodate
accommodated
accommodating
accommodation
accommodation bill
accompanied
accompany
accompanying
accomplice
accomplish
accomplished
accomplishment
accord
accord and
   satisfaction
accordance
according
accordingly
accost
account
account charge and
   discharge
account of charge and
   discharge
accountable
accountant
Accountant of Court

accounting
accredited
accresce
accretion
accrue
accrued
accruing
accumulate
accumulated
accumulating
accumulation
accumulation and
   maintenance
   settlement
accumulator
accuracy
accurate
accurately
accusation
accuse
accused
accuser
accusing
accustomed
acetylene
ache
ached
achieve
achieved
achievement
achieving
aching
acknowledge
acknowledged
acknowledgement
acknowledging
acquaint
acquaintance
acquiesce
acquiesced
acquiescence
acquiescing

acquire
acquired
acquired immune
  deficiency
  syndrome (AIDS)
acquiring
acquisition
acquisitive
acquit
acquittal
acquittance
acquitted
acquitting
acre
acreage
acrimonious
acrimony
acronym
across
acrylic
act
act and warrant
act of God
Act of Parliament
acte clair
actings
actio in personam
actio personalis
  moritur cum
  persona
action
action of count
  reckoning and
  payment
action of exhibition
action of furthcoming
actionable
actions civil and penal
activate
activated
activating
active

active trust
active trustee
actively
activities
activity
Acts of Adjournal
Acts of Sederunt
actual
actually
actuaries
actuary
actuate
actuated
actuating
actus non facit reum
  nisi mens sit rea
actus reus
acumen
acute
acutely
acuteness
ad colligenda bona
ad diem
ad factum
  praestandum
ad fundandam
  jurisdictionem
ad hoc
ad huc
ad idem
ad infinitum
ad interim
ad litem
ad longum
ad omissa velmale
  appretiata
ad perpetuam
  remanentiam
ad rem
ad valorem
ad vitam aut culpam
adamant

adapt
adaptable
adaptation
add
added
addenda
addendum
addict
addicted
addiction
addictive
adding
addition
additional
additionally
address
addressed
addressee
addresses
addressing
adduce
ademption
adept
adequacy
adequate
adequately
adhere
adhered
adherence
adherent
adhering
adhesion
adhesive
adjacent
adjoin
adjoined
adjoining
adjourn
adjournment
adjudicate
adjudicated
adjudicating

adjudication
adjudicator
adjunct
adjust
adjustable
adjustment
adminicle
administer
administered
administering
administrate
administrated
administrating
administration
administrative
administrator
administrator in law
admirable
admirably
Admiralty Court
Admiralty proceedings
admiration
admire
admired
admiring
admissible
admissible evidence
admissibly
admission
admit
admittance
admitted
admitting
admonish
admonished
admonition
admonitory
adolescence
adolescent
adopt
adopted as holograph
adoption

adoption order
adoptive
adroit
adult
adulterate
adulterated
adulterating
adulteration
adulterer
adulteress
adulteresses
adultery
advance
advanced
advancement
advancing
advantage
advantageous
adventitious
adversaries
adversary
adverse
adverse occupation
adversely
adversities
adversity
advertent negligence
advertise
advertised
advertisement
advertising
advice
advice on evidence
advisability
advisable
advise
advised
advising
advisory
Advisory, Conciliation
   and Arbitration
   Service (ACAS)

advocate
advocated
advocate-depute
Advocate-General
advocating
advowson
aedificatum solo, solo
   cedit
aemulatio vicini
aequitas est quasi
   aequalitas
aerial
aerodrome
aeroplane
aerosol
affair
affect
affectation
affidavit
affiliate
affiliated
affiliating
affiliation
affiliation order
affinities
affinity
affirm
affirmanti non neganti
   incumbit probatio
affirmation
affirmative
affirmative pregnant
affix
afflict
affliction
affluence
affluent
afford
afforestation
affray
affrayed
affreightment

Aa

affront
afloat
afoot
aforesaid
afraid
after
after care condition
aftermath
afternoon
afterthought
afterwards
again
against
age
age of consent
aged
ageing
agencies
agency
agenda
agent
agent provocateur
aggravate
aggravated
aggravated assault
aggravated burglary
aggravating
aggravation
aggregate
aggression
aggressive
aggressively
aggrieved
aggrieved person
aging
agistment
agnate
agnostic
agnosticism
ago
agony
agoraphobia

agree
agreeable
agreeably
agreed
agreeing
agreement
agricultural
agricultural holding
agricultural tenancy
agriculturally
agriculture
aground
ague
ahead
aid
aid and abet
aim
aimless
airborne
aircraft
airport
airspace
akin
alarm
alarming
alarmist
albeit
alcohol
alcoholic
alcoholism
alderman
aleatory contract
alert
alias
aliases
alibi
alien
alienable
alienate
alienated
alienating
alienation

alieni juris
alight
alighted
alighting
align
aligned
aligning
alignment
alike
aliment
alimentary
alimentary provision
alimentary trust
alimony
alit
aliter
alive
all fours
all right
allay
allayed
allaying
allegation
allege
alleged
allegiance
alleging
allenarly
allergic
allergies
allergy
alleviate
alleviated
alleviating
alleviation
alliance
allied
allies
allocate
allocated
allocating
allocation

5

Aa

allocatur
allocutus
allodial
allodial land
allot
allotment
allotted
allotting
allow
allowable
allowance
allowed
allowing
all-risks policy
allude
alluded
alluding
allusion
alluvion
ally
allying
almost
alone
along
aloof
aloofness
aloud
already
also
altar
alter
alteration
altercation
altered
altering
alternate
alternated
alternately
alternating
alternative
alternatively
although

altitude
altius non tollendi
altogether
altruism
altruistic
altruistically
always
am
amalgam
amalgamate
amalgamated
amalgamating
amalgamation
amass
amateur
amateurish
amaze
amazed
amazement
amazing
ambassador
ambassadress
ambassadresses
ambidexterous
ambidextrous
ambiguities
ambiguity
ambiguous
ambition
ambitious
ambulance
ambulatory
ambush
ambushes
amenable
amend
amendment
amenities
amenity
amercement
American
amiable

amiably
amicable
amicably
amicus curiae
amid
amidst
amiss
ammunition
amnesia
amnesties
amnesty
amok
among
amongst
amoral
amorous
amorousness
amount
ample
amplification
amplified
amplifier
amplify
amplifying
amplitude
amply
amputate
amputated
amputating
amputation
amuck
amuse
amused
amusement
amusing
anachronism
anachronistic
anaemia
anaemic
anaesthetic
anaesthetist
analogies

analogous
analogue
analogy
analyse
analysed
analyses
analysing
analysis
anarchist
anarchy
anathema
anatomical
anatomically
anatomist
anatomy
ancestor
ancestral
ancestress
ancestresses
ancestry
anchor
anchorage
anchored
anchoring
ancient
ancient document
ancient lights
ancient monument
ancillary
ancillary credit
   business
ancillary probate
ancillary relief
anecdotal
anecdote
anger
angered
angering
angina
angle
angled
Anglican

anglicize
anglicized
anglicizing
angling
Anglo-Saxon
angrily
angry
anguish
anguished
angular
animal
animate
animated
animating
animation
animosity
animus
animus furandi
animus non revertendi
animus possidendi
animus testandi
ankle
annals
annex
annexe
annihilate
annihilated
annihilating
annihilation
anniversaries
anniversary
annotate
annotated
annotating
annotation
announce
announced
announcement
announcer
announcing
annoy
annoyance

annoyed
annoying
annual
annual rent
annual return
annually
annuities
annuity
annul
annulled
annulling
annulment
anomalies
anomalous
anomaly
anonymity
anonymous
another
Ansafone®
answer
answerable
answered
answering
antagonism
antagonist
antagonistic
antagonistically
antagonize
antagonized
antagonizing
Antarctic
ante litem motam
antecedent
antecedent
   negotiations
antecedent rights
ante-date
antediluvian
antenatal
antenna
antennae
antennas

antibiotic
anticipate
anticipated
anticipating
anticipation
anticipatory breach
anticlimax
anticlockwise
anti-competitive
  practice
antidote
antipathy
antiquated
antique
antiseptic
antisocial
antitheses
antithesis
Anton Piller order
anxieties
anxiety
anxious
any
anybody
anyhow
anyone
anything
anywhere
apart
apartheid
apathetic
apathetically
apathy
aplomb
apocha trium annorum
apocryphal
apologetic
apologetically
apologies
apologize
apologized
apologizing

apology
apostrophe
appal
appalled
appalling
apparatus
apparel
apparent
apparently
appeal
appealed
appealing
appear
appearance
appeared
appearing
appease
appeased
appeasing
appellant
appellate jurisdiction
append
appendant
appendicitis
appendix
appertain
appertained
appertaining
appetite
appliance
applicable
applicant
application
applied
apply
applying
appoint
appointee
appointment
appointor
apportion
apportioned

apportioning
apportionment
apposite
appraisal
appraise
appraised
appraiser
appraising
appreciable
appreciably
appreciate
appreciated
appreciating
appreciation
apprehend
apprehension
apprehensive
apprehensively
apprentice
apprenticeship
apprise
approach
approachable
approaches
approbate
approbate and
  reprobate
approbation
appropriate
appropriate in aid
appropriated
appropriately
appropriating
appropriation
approval
approve
approved
approvement
approving
approximate
approximately
approximation

approximation of laws
appurtenant
apropos of
apt
aptitude
aptly
apud acta
aqua cedit solo
aquaeductus
aquaehaustus
aqueduct
arable
arbiter
arbitrage
arbitrarily
arbitrary
arbitrate
arbitrated
arbitrating
arbitration
arbitration agreement
arbitration and interest
arbitration clause
arbitrator
arc
arch
archaeological
archaeologist
archaeology
archaic
archbishop
arches
architect
architectural
architecturally
architecture
archives
Arctic
arduous
arduousness
are
area

arena
aren't
arguable
arguably
argue
argued
arguendo
arguing
argument
argumentative
argumentative
 affidavit
argumentatively
arise
arisen
arising
aristocracy
aristocrat
aristocratic
aristocratically
arithmetic
arithmetical
arithmetically
arles
armaments
armed
armistice
arm's length
arose
around
arouse
aroused
arousing
arraign
arraignment
arrange
arranged
arrangement
arranging
array
arrears
arrest

arrest and warrant
arrest of judgement
arrest of ship
arrestable offence
arrestee
arrestment
arrestment in
 execution
arrestment on the
 dependence
arrestment to found
 jurisdiction
arrestor
arrival
arrive
arrived
arrived ship
arriving
arrogance
arrogant
arsenal
arsenic
arson
arsonist
art and part
arterial
arteries
artery
artful
artfully
article
articles of association
Articles of Roup
articulate
articulated
articulating
articulation
artificial
artificial insemination
 (AID)
artificial person
artificiality

artificially
artisan
artist
artiste
artistic
artistically
artistry
artless
as accords of law
as effeirs
asbestos
ascend
ascendancy
ascendant
ascended
ascendency
ascendent
ascending
ascent
ascertain
ascertained goods
ascetic
ascetically
ascribe
ascribed
ascribing
ashamed
ashore
aside
asinine
ask
askance
askew
asleep
aspect
asperity
asphalt
asphyxia
asphyxiate
asphyxiated
asphyxiating
asphyxiation

aspiration
aspire
aspired
aspirin
aspiring
asportation
assail
assailant
assailed
assailing
assassin
assassinate
assassinated
assassinating
assassination
assault
assemble
assembled
assemblies
assembling
assembly
assent
assert
assertion
assertive
assertively
assess
assessment
assessor
asset
assiduous
assign
assignable
assignation
assigned
assignee
assigning
assignment
assignment of lease
assignor
assimilate
assimilated

assimilating
assimilation
assist
assistance
assistant
assize
associate
associated
associated employers
associating
association
assoilzie
assorted
assortment
assuage
assuaged
assuaging
assume
assumed
assuming
assumpsit
assumption
assurance
assure
assured
assuring
asterisk
asthma
asthmatic
astonish
astonishment
astound
astray
astride
astute
asylum
ate
atmosphere
atmospheric
atmospherically
atone
atoned

atonement
atoning
atrocious
atrocities
atrocity
attach
attaché-case
attached
attaching
attachment
attack
attacker
attain
attainable
attainder
attainment
attaint
attempt
attend
attendance
attendant
attention
attentive
attentively
attest
attestation
attire
attired
attiring
attitude
attorney
Attorney-General
 (A-G)
attornment
attour
attract
attraction
attractive
attractively
attributable
attribute
attributed

attributing
au fait
auction
auctioneer
auctor in rem suam
audacious
audacity
audi alteram partem
audibility
audible
audibly
audience
audio-typist
audio-visual
audit
audited
auditing
auditor
auditor of court
auditory
augment
augmentation
augur
augured
auguring
August
aural
auspices
auspicious
austere
austerely
austerity
Australian
Austrian
authentic
authenticate
authenticated
authenticating
authentication
authenticity
author
authorised capital

authorised securities
authoritarian
authoritative
authorities
authority
authorization
authorize
authorized
authorizing
autograph
automata
automatic
automatically
automation
automatism
automaton
autonomic legislation
autonomous
autonomy
autopsies
autopsy
autre vie
autrefois acquit
autrefois convict
autumn
autumnal
auxiliaries
auxiliary
avail
availability
available
availed
availing
avarice
avaricious
avenge
avenged
avenger
avenging
avenue
aver
average

averaged
averaging
averment
averse
aversion
avert
aviation
aviator
avid
avidity
avizandum
avoid
avoidable
avoidably
avoidance
avoirdupois
avow
avowal
avulsio
avulsion
await
awake
awaken
awakened
awakening
award
aware
awareness
away
awful
awfully
awfulness
awkward
awkwardly
awkwardness
awoke
awry
axe
axed
axes
axing
axis
axle

Bb

babies
baby
babyhood
bachelor
bachelorhood
back
back letter
back up
back-bond
backed for bail
backer
background
backhand rent
backing
backward
bacteria
bacterial
bacteriologist
bacteriology
bad
bad debt
bade
badger
badgered
badgering
baffle
baffled
baffling
bag
baggage
bagged
bagging
bail
bail with sureties
bailable
bailed
bailee
bailie

bailiff
bailment
bailor
bairns' part
bait
baited
baiting
balance
balance of
    probabilities
balance sheet
balanced
balancing
balconies
balcony
bald
bale
bale out
baled out
baleful
balefully
baling
baling out
balk
balked
balking
ballast
ballistic
ballot
balustrade
ban
banal
banalities
banality
band
bandage
bandaged
bandaging
bandied
bandy
bandying
bane

banish
banishment
banister
bank
banker
banking instrument
bank-note
bankrupt
bankruptcy
banned
banner
banning
banns
bans
banter
bantering
baptism
baptismal
baptize
baptized
baptizing
bar
Bar Council
barb
barbarian
barbaric
barbarically
barbarities
barbarity
barbed
barber
bare
bare licensee
bare site value
bare trust
bared
barely
bareness
bargain
bargained
bargaining
barge

barged
barging
baring
barometer
Baron (B)
baroness
baronesses
baronet
baronetcy
barony
barracks
barrage
barred
barrel
barren
barrenness
barricade
barricaded
barricading
barrier
barring
barring of entailed
    interest
barrister
barter
bartered
bartering
base
base fee
base holding
based
basement
basic
basic intent
basically
basin
basing
basis
bastard
bastion
batch
batches

bated
baton
battalion
batter
battered
batteries
battering
battery
battle
battled
battling
bauble
baulk
baulked
baulking
be
beach
beam
bear
bearable
beard
bearded
bearer
bearer shares
bearing
beast
beastliness
beastly
beat
beaten
beauties
beautified
beautiful
beautifully
beautify
beautifying
beauty
becalmed
became
because
beckon
beckoned

Bb

beckoning
become
becoming
bed
bedded
bedding
Beddoe order
bedlam
bedraggled
bedridden
bed-sit
bed-sitter
been
befall
befallen
befalling
befell
befit
befitted
befitting
before
beforehand
befriend
beg
began
beget
beggar
beggared
beggaring
beggarly
begged
begging
begin
beginning
begot
begotten
begrudge
begrudged
begrudging
beguile
beguiled
beguiling

begun
behalf
behave
behaved
behaving
behaviour
behead
behest
behind
beholden
being
belabour
belaboured
belabouring
belated
Belgian
belie
belied
belief
believe
believed
believing
belittle
belittled
belittling
bell
belle
bellicose
bellies
belligerent
belly
belong
belonged
belonging
beloved
below
belying
bench
bench warrant
Benchers
benches
bend

bending
beneath
benediction
benefactor
benefice
beneficial freehold
  owner
beneficial interest
beneficially
beneficiaries
beneficiary
beneficium
beneficium ordinis
benefit
benefited
benefiting
Benelux
benevolence
benevolent
benevolent society
benign
Benjamin order
bent
bequeath
bequeathed
bequeathing
bequest
berate
berated
berating
bereaved
bereavement
bereft
berserk
berth
berthed
berthing
beseech
beset
besetting
beside
besides

besiege
besieged
besieging
best
bestial
bestiality
bestially
bestow
bet
bête noire
betray
betrayal
betrayed
betraying
betrothal
betrothed
betted
better
bettered
bettering
betterment
betting
between
beverage
beware
bewilder
bewildered
bewildering
beyond
beyond reasonable
    doubt
beyond the seas
bias
biased
biasing
biassed
biassing
bible
biblical
bibliographer
bibliographies
bibliography

bicentenary
bicker
bickered
bickering
bicycle
bid
bidding
biennial
biennially
bier
big
bigamist
bigamous
bigamy
bigger
biggest
bigot
bigoted
bigotry
bilateral
bilateral contract
bilateral discharge
bile
bilingual
bilious
biliousness
bill
bill of costs
bill of exchange
bill of indictment
bill of lading
bill of sale
billet
billet-doux
billeted
billeting
billets-doux
billion
binary
bind
bind over
binding

binoculars
biographer
biographical
biographies
biography
biological
biologically
biologist
biology
bird
Biro®
birth
birth certificate
birthday
bisect
bishop
bishopric
bit
bitch
bitches
bite
bitten
bitter
bi-weekly
bizarre
black
blackboard
blacken
blackened
blackening
blackguard
blackleg
blackmail
blackmailed
blackmailer
blackmailing
bladder
blade
blame
blamed
blameless
blaming

bland
blandishments
blank
blank transfer
blanket
blanketed
blanketing
blare
blared
blaring
blarney
blaspheme
blasphemed
blaspheming
blasphemous
blasphemy
blast
blast-off
blatant
blaze
blazed
blazing
blazon
blazoned
blazoning
bleak
bleakness
bleary
bleat
bled
bleed
bleeding
blemish
blemishes
blench
bless
blessed
blessing
blew
blight
blight notice
blind

blindfold
blindness
blister
blistered
blistering
blithe
blithely
blitz
blizzard
bloated
bloc
block
block grant
blockade
blockaded
blockading
blood
blood relationship
blood test
bloodhound
bloodshed
bloody
bloom
bloomed
blooming
blossom
blossomed
blossoming
blot
blotted
blotter
blotting
blouse
blow
blowing
blown
blowy
bludgeon
bludgeoned
bludgeoning
blue
blue book

blue chip
blueprint
bluff
blunder
blundered
blundering
blunt
blur
blurred
blurring
blurt out
blush
blushes
bluster
blustered
blustering
board
board meeting
board of directors
boarder
boast
boastful
boastfully
boat
boating
boatswain
bob
bobbed
bobbing
bode
boded
bodice
bodily
boding
body
body corporate
bodyguard
bog down
bogged down
bogging down
bogus
boil

boiled
boiler
boiling
boisterous
bold
bollard
bolster up
bolstered up
bolstering up
bolt
bomb
bomb hoax
bombard
bombardment
bombastic
bombed
bomber
bombing
bombshell
bona fide
bona fides
bona mobilia
bona vacantia
bond
bond and disposition
   in security
bondage
bonded warehouse
bone
bonus
bonus shares
bonuses
bony
book
book debt
bookie
bookkeeping
booklet
books of account
Books of Adjournal
Books of Council and
   Session

Books of Sederunt
boom
boomed
booming
boon
boor
boorish
boost
booster
booth
booty
border
bordered
bordering
bore
bored
boredom
boring
born
borne
borough
borrow
Borstal institution
bosom
boss
bosses
bosun
bote
both
bother
bothered
bothering
bottle
bottled
bottleneck
bottling
bottom
bough
bought
bought as seen
boulder
boulevard

bounce
bounced
bouncer
bouncing
bound
boundaries
boundary
boundary commission
bounded
bounding
boundless
bounties
bounty
bourgeois
bourse
bout
bovine
bow
bowels
bowed
bowing
box
boxer
boxes
boy
boycott
boycotted
boycotting
boyhood
brace
braced
bracing
bracket
bracketed
bracketing
brae
brag
bragged
bragging
braid
braille
brain

Bb

brained
braining
brainwave
brainy
brake
braked
braking
branch
branches
brand
brandies
brandish
brandy
brassy
bravado
brave
braved
bravely
bravery
braving
brawl
brawn
brawny
brazen
brazen it out
brazened it out
brazening it out
breach
breach of close
breach of confidence
breach of contract
breach of privilege
breach of statutory
  duty
breach of the peace
breach of trust
breaches
breadth
breadwinner
break
breakable
breakage

breaker
breakfast
break-in
breaking
breaking and entering
breast
breath
breath test
breathalyser
breathe
breathed
breathing
breathless
bred
breech
breeches
breed
breeding
brevi manu
brevitatis causa
brevity
brew
breweries
brewery
brewster sessions
bribe
bribed
bribery
bribing
brick
bridge
bridged
bridging
bridging loan
bridle
bridled
bridleway
bridling
brief
brieve
brigade
brigand

bright
brighten
brightened
brightening
brilliance
brilliant
brim
brimful
brimmed
brimming
bring
bringing
brink
brisk
bristle
bristled
bristling
bristly
Britain
British
British citizen
British citizenship
British Commonwealth
British protected
  person
British protectorate
Briton
brittle
broach
broached
broaching
broad
broadcast
broadcasting
broaden
broadened
broadening
brocard
brogue
broke
broken
broker

brokerage
bronchitic
brooch
brooches
brood
brook
brothel
brother
brotherhood
brother-in-law
brotherly
brought
brow
browbeat
browbeating
brown
browse
browsed
browsing
bruise
bruised
bruising
brunt
brush
brushes
brusque
brusquely
brusqueness
brutal
brutality
brutally
brute
brutish
brutum fulmen
bubble
bubbled
bubbling
bubbly
buck
bucket
buckle
buckled

buckler
buckling
Buddhism
Buddhist
budge
budged
budget
budgetary
budgeted
budgeting
budging
buff
buffer
buffoon
buffoonery
bug
bugbear
bugged
buggery
bugging
build
builder
building
building lease
building scheme
building society
building society
  advance
built
built-up
bulbous
bulge
bulged
bulging
bulk
bulky
bulldoze
bulldozed
bulldozer
bulldozing
bullet
bulletin

bullied
bullies
bullion
Bullock order
bull's-eye
bully
bullying
bulwark
bump
bumper
bumpkin
bumptious
bumptiousness
bunch
bunches
bundle
bundled
bundling
bungalow
bungle
bungled
bungling
bunk
bunk-bed
bunker
buoy
buoyancy
buoyant
burden
burden of proof
burdened
burdening
bureau
bureaucracies
bureaucracy
bureaucratic
bureaus
bureaux
burgage
burgh
burglar
burglaries

burglary
burgle
burgled
burgling
burial
buried
burly
burn
burned
burner
burning
burnish
burnt
burrow
burst
bursting
bury
burying
bus
buses
bush
bushes
bushy
busier
busiest
busily
business
business day
business liability
business name
business tenancy
businesses
businessman
bust
bustle
bustled
bustling
busy
but
butcher
butler
butt

buttocks
button
buttoned
buttonhole
buttoning
buttress
buttresses
buxom
buy
buyer
buying
by
bye-law
by-election
bygone
by-law
bypass
bypassed
bypassing
by-product
bystander

Cc

cab
cabin
Cabinet
cable
cabled
cabling
cache
cacophonous
cacophony
cacti
cactus
cactuses
cad
cadaverous
cadence

cadet
cadge
cadged
cadger
cadging
café
cafeteria
caffeine
cage
caged
cagey
caging
cagy
cajole
cajoled
cajoling
calamine
calamities
calamitous
calamity
calcium
calculate
calculated
calculating
calculation
calculator
Calderbank letter
calendar
calibrate
calibrated
calibrating
calibre
calipers
call
called up capital
calligraphy
calling the jury
callipers
callous
callow
calluses
calm

calmness
calorie
calumnies
calumny
camber
came
cameo
camera
camouflage
camouflaged
camouflaging
camp
campaign
campaigned
campaigning
camping
campsite
campus
campuses
can
canal
cancel
cancellation
cancelled
cancelling
cancer
cancerous
candid
candidacy
candidate
candle
Candlemas
candlestick
candour
cane
caned
canine
caning
canister
canker
cannabis
canned

canneries
cannery
canning
cannot
canoe
canon
canon law
canonical disability
canopies
canopy
cant
can't
cantankerous
canted
canter
cantered
cantering
canting
canvas
canvases
canvass
canvassed
canvassing
cap
capabilities
capability
capable
capacious
capacities
capacity
capacity to contract
cape
caper
capered
capering
capias
capillaries
capillary
capital
capital allowances
capital clause
capital gains tax

capital money
capital punishment
capital redemption
    reserve
capital reserve
capital transfer tax
capital-intensive
capitalisation
capitalism
capitalist
capitalistic
capitalization
capitalize
capitalized
capitalizing
capitulate
capitulated
capitulating
capitulation
capped
capping
caprice
capricious
capricious power
capsize
capsized
capsizing
capstan
capsule
captain
captaincies
captaincy
captained
captaining
caption
captious
captivate
captivated
captivating
captive
captivity
captor

capture
captured
capturing
car
carafe
carat
caravan
carbohydrate
carbolic
carbon
carburetter
carcase
carcass
card
cardboard
cardiac
care
care and control
care proceedings
cared
career
careered
careering
carefree
careful
carefully
carefulness
careless
carelessness
caress
caressed
caresses
caressing
caretaker
cargo
cargoes
caricature
caricaturist
caring
carnage
carnal knowledge
carnivore

carnivorous
carouse
caroused
carousing
carp
carpenter
carpentry
carpet
carpeted
carpeting
carriage
carriageway
carried
carrier
carrier's lien
carry
carrying
cart
carte blanche
cartel
cartilage
cartridge
carve
carved
carving
cascade
cascaded
cascading
case
case law
case stated
cased
casement
cash
cash credit
cashier
cashiered
cashiering
casing
casino
cask
casket

cassette
cast
caste
castigate
castigated
castigating
casting
cast-off
castrate
castrated
castrating
casual
casually
casualties
casualty
casus amissionis
casus belli
casus omissus
cat
cataclysm
catalogue
catalogued
cataloguing
catalyst
catapult
cataract
catarrh
catastrophe
catastrophic
catastrophically
catch
catching
catching bargain
catchment
catechism
categorical
categorically
categories
category
cater
catered
caterer

catering
caterwauling
cathedral
cathode ray tube
catholic
Catholic
catholic creditor
cattle
cattle trespass
caught
causa
causa causans
causa proxima et non
    remota spectatur
causa remota
causa sine qua non
causation
cause
cause of action
caused
causeway
causing
caustic
caustically
cauterize
cauterized
cauterizing
caution
cautionary
cautioner
cautious
cavalier
cave
cave in
caveat
caveat emptor
caveat venditor
caved in
cavern
cavernous
cavil
cavilled

cavilling
caving in
cavities
cavity
cavort
cease
ceased
ceaseless
ceasing
cede
ceded
cedent
ceding
Ceefax®
ceiling
celebrate
celebrated
celebrating
celebration
celebrities
celebrity
celibacy
celibate
cell
cellophane
Celsius
cement
cemeteries
cemetery
censor
censored
censoring
censorious
censure
censured
censuring
census
censuses
cent
centenaries
centenary
centigrade

centigram
centigramme
centilitre
centimetre
central
Central Criminal Court
centralization
centralize
centralized
centralizing
centrally
centre
centrifugal
centuries
century
cerebral
ceremonial
ceremonies
ceremonious
ceremony
certain
certainly
certainties
certainty
certificate
certificate of shares
certificate of
    incorporation
certificate to
    commence
    business
certification
Certification Officer
certified
certify
certifying
certiorari
certiorate
certum est quod
    certum reddi potest
cessante ratione legis,
    cessat ipsa lex

cessate grant
cessation
cesser
cesser clause
cestui que trust
cestui que use
cestui que vie
ceteris paribus
chagrin
chain
chain of title
chain of
   representation
chained
chaining
chair
chaired
chairing
chairman
chalk
chalky
challenge
challenged
challenging
chamber
chamberlain
chameleon
champion
championed
championing
championship
chance
chanced
chancellor
Chancellor (C)
chancery
Chancery Division
Chancery Masters
chancing
change
change of voyage
changeable

changed
changing
channel
channelled
channelling
chant
chaos
chaotic
chaotically
chap
chapel
chaperone
chaperoned
chaperoning
chaplain
chapter
char
character
characteristic
characteristically
characterization
characterize
characterized
characterizing
charade
charcoal
charge
chargeable
charged
charger
Charges Register
charging
charging clause
charging order
charitable
charitable trust
charitably
charities
charity
Charity
   Commissioners
charlatan

charm
charming
charred
charring
chart
charted
charter
Charter of
   Novodamus
charter party
chartered
chartering
charterparty
charterparty by way of
   demise
charting
chartulary
charwoman
chary
chase
chased
chasing
chasm
chaste
chasten
chastened
chastening
chastise
chastised
chastisement
chastising
chastity
chat
chatted
chattels
chattels
chattels personal
chattels real
chatter
chattered
chattering
chattily

chatting
chatty
chauffeur
cheap
cheapen
cheapened
cheapening
cheat
check
checked
check-out
cheer
cheered
cheerful
cheerfully
cheerily
cheering
cheery
chef
chemical
chemically
chemist
chemistry
cheque
cheque card
chequered
cherish
chest
chew
chic
chicanery
chid
chide
chided
chiding
chief
Chief Baron of the
    Exchequer (CB)
Chief Justice (CJ)
Chief Justice of the
    Court of Common
    Pleas (CJCP)

Chief Justice of the
    Court of King's
    Bench (CJKB)
chief rent
chiefly
chieftain
chilblain
child
child abuse
child benefit
child destruction
child of the family
childbirth
childhood
childish
childlike
childminder
children
children's hearing
children's panel
chill
Chiltern Hundreds
chime
chimed
chiming
chimney
chin
china
Chinese
chink
chintz
chip
chipped
chipping
chirograph
chirographum apud
    debitorem repertum
chiropodist
chiropody
chisel
chiselled
chiselling

chit
chivalrous
chivalry
chlorinate
chlorinated
chlorinating
chlorine
chloroform
choice
choke
choked
choking
cholera
choose
choosing
chop
chopped
chopper
chopping
choppy
chore
chorus
choruses
chose
chose in action
chosen
christen
christened
christening
Christian
Christianity
Christmas
Christmas Day
chrome
chromium
chronic
chronically
chronicle
chronicler
chronological
chronologically
chunk

church
churches
churlish
churn
chute
cigarette
cinema
cipher
circa
circle
circled
circling
circuit
circuit court
circuit judge
circuit system
circuitous
circuity of action
circular
circulate
circulated
circulating
circulation
circumference
circumlocution
circumspect
circumstances
circumstantial
circumstantial
  evidence
circumstantiate
circumstantiated
circumstantiating
circumvent
circumvention
cistern
citation
cite
cited
cities
citing
citizen

citizen's arrest
citizenship
citizenship by descent
city
civic
civil
civil action
civil appeal
civil commotion
civil debt
civil law
Civil List
civil marriage
civil remedy
Civil Service
civilian
civilities
civility
civilization
civilize
civilized
civilizing
civilly
clad
claim
claimant
claimed
claiming
clairvoyance
clairvoyant
clam up
clamber
clambered
clambering
clameur de haro
clammed up
clamming up
clamorous
clamour
clamp
clan
clandestine

clandestinely
clannish
clap
clapped
clapping
clare constat
clarified
clarify
clarifying
clarity
clash
clashes
class
class gift
class rights
classes
classic
classical
classically
classification
classified
classify
classifying
clatter
clattered
clattering
clause
clause of devolution
clause of return
claustrophobia
claustrophobic
claw
clay
clean
clean hands
cleaned
cleaner
cleaning
cleanliness
cleanness
cleanse
cleansed

cleansing
clear
clear days
clearance
clearance area
cleared
clearing
clearly
clearness
cleavage
cleave
cleaver
cleft
clemency
clement
clench
clergy
clergyman
clerical
clerk
Clerk of Justiciary
Clerk of Session
Clerk of Teinds
Clerk to the Signet
clever
cleverness
cliché
click
client
clientele
cliff
climate
climatic
climax
climaxes
climb
climber
clinch
clinches
cling
clinging
clinic

clinical
clinically
clip
clipped
clipping
clique
cloak
clock
clockwise
clockwork
clod
clog
clogged
clogging
cloister
cloistered
close
close company
close season
closed
closed record
closed-shop
    agreement
closely
closeness
closet
closet with
closeted with
closeting with
close-up
closing
closing order
closing speeches
closure
clot
cloth
clothe
clothed
clothes
clothing
cloths
clotted

clotting
cloud
cloudy
cloy
cloyed
cloying
club
clubbed
clubbing
clue
clumsily
clumsiness
clumsy
clung
cluster
clustered
clustering
clutch
clutches
clutter
cluttered
cluttering
co
coach
coaches
coagulate
coagulated
coagulating
coal
coalesce
coalesced
coalescing
coalfield
coalition
coarse
coarsely
coarsen
coarsened
coarseness
coarsening
coast
coastal

coastal waters
coaster
coastguard
coat
coated
coating
coax
cobble
cobbled
cobbler
cobbling
cocaine
cock
cockily
cockpit
cockroach
cockroaches
cocktail
cocky
coddle
coddled
coddling
code
code of practice
codicil
codifying statute
co-driver
coeducation
coerce
coerced
coercing
coercion
coercive
co-exist
co-existence
coffer
coffin
cog
cogency
cogent
cogitate
cogitated

cogitating
cognac
cognate
cognition
cognitionis causa
   tantum
cognizance
cohabit
cohabitation
co-heir
cohere
cohered
coherence
coherent
cohering
cohesion
cohesive
cohort
coiffure
coil
coiled
coiling
coin
coinage
coincide
coincided
coincidence
coincidental
coinciding
coined
coining
cold
coldness
colic
collaborate
collaborated
collaborating
collaboration
collaborator
collapse
collapsed
collapsible

collapsing
collar
collarbone
collared
collaring
collate
collated
collateral
collateral relationship
collateral security
collating
collatio inter haeredes
collatio inter liberos
collation
colleague
collect
collection
collective
collective bargaining
collectively
collective
   responsibility
collector
college
College of Justice
collegiate
collide
collided
colliding
collier
collieries
colliery
collision
colloquial
colloquialism
colloquially
collude
collusion
collusive
colon
colonel
colonial

colonist
colonization
colonize
colonized
colonizing
colony
colore officii
colossal
colour
coloured
colourful
colourfully
colouring
colourless
column
coma
comatose
comb
combat
combatant
combated
combating
combination
combine
combined
combining
combustible
combustion
come
comedian
comedies
comedy
comfort
comfortable
comfortably
comic
comical
comically
coming
comity
comma
command

Command Papers
(Cd; Cm; Cmd;
Cmnd)
commandeer
commandeered
commandeering
commander
commandment
commando
commandoes
commemorate
commemorated
commemorating
commemoration
commence
commenced
commencement
commencing
commend
commendable
commendation
commensurate
comment
commentaries
commentary
commentator
commerce
commercial
Commercial Court
commercially
commiserate
commiserated
commiserating
commiseration
commissariat
commissary
Commissary Court
commission
Commission for Racial
Equality
commission for taking
proof

Commission of
Review
commissionaire
commissioned
commissioner
Commissioner for
Local Administration
Commissioner for
Oaths
Commissioners of
Inland Revenue
Commissioners of
Teinds
commissioning
commit
commit to custody
commitment
committal
committal for trial
committal for
sentence
committal proceedings
committed
committee
committing
commixtion
commodate
commodious
commodities
commodity
common
common agent
common assault
common calamity
common carrier
common debtor
common good
common interest
common land
common law
Common Market
common property

commoner
common-law marriage
commonplace
commonty
Commonwealth
commorientes
commotion
communal
commune
communed
communicate
communicated
communicating
communication
communicative
communing
communion
communiqué
communis error facit
   jus
communism
communist
communities
community
community charge
community council
community home
Community law
community service
   order
commutative contract
commutative justice
commute
commuted
commuter
commuting
compact
companies
Companies Court
companies register
companion
companionable

companionably
company
company accounts
company arrangement
company name
company secretary
company's common
   seal
company's official
   seal
comparable
comparably
comparative
comparatively
compare
compared
comparing
comparison
compartment
compass
compasses
compassion
compassionate
compassionately
compatibility
compatible
compatibly
compatriot
compear
compearance
compel
compelled
compelling
compensate
compensated
compensating
compensatio
   injuriarum
compensation
compete
competed
competence

competent
competent and
   omitted
competing
competition
competition law
competitive
competitor
compilation
compile
compiled
compiler
compiling
complacency
complacent
complain
complainant
complained
complaining
complaint
complement
complementary
complete
completed
completely
completely constituted
   trust
completeness
completing
completion
complex
complexes
complexion
complexities
complexity
compliance
compliant
complicate
complicated
complicating
complication
complicity

complied
compliment
complimentary
comply
complying
component
compos mentis
compose
composed
composing
composite
composition
composition contract
compositor
composure
compound
compound settlement
comprehend
comprehensible
comprehension
comprehensive
comprehensively
compress
compression
comprise
comprised
comprising
compromise
compromised
compromising
comptroller
compulsion
compulsive
compulsively
compulsorily
compulsory
compulsory purchase
 order
compulsory winding-
 up
compunction
computation

compute
computed
computer
computing
comrade
con
concave
conceal
concealed
concealed fraud
concealing
concealment
concede
conceded
conceding
conceit
conceited
conceivable
conceivably
conceive
conceived
conceiving
concentrate
concentrated
concentrating
concentration
concentric
concept
conception
concern
concerning
concert party
concerted
concession
conciliate
conciliated
conciliating
conciliation
conciliatory
concise
conciseness
conclude

concluded
concluding
conclusion
conclusive
conclusive evidence
conclusively
concoct
concoction
concord
concourse
concrete
concubinage
concur
concurred
concurrence
concurrent
concurrent interests
concurrent lease
concurrent sentences
concurrent tortfeasors
concurring
concursus debiti et
 crediti
concussion
condemn
condemnation
condemned
condemning
condensation
condense
condensed
condensing
condescend
condescendence
condescending
condescension
conditio si institutus
 sine liberis
 decesserit
conditio si testator
 sine liberis
 decesserit

condition
condition concurrent
condition precedent
condition subsequent
conditional
conditional
  acceptance
conditional
  admissibility
conditional agreement
conditional discharge
conditional
  endorsement
conditional institute
conditionally
conditioned
conditioning
conditions in deed
conditions of sale
condole
condoled
condolences
condoling
condonation
condone
condoned
condoning
conducive
conduct
conduction
conductor
conductress
conductresses
conduit
confederacy
confederate
confederation
confer
conference
conferred
conferring
confess

confessing error
confession
confession and
  avoidance
confession of defence
confidant
confidante
confide
confided
confidence
confident
confidential
confidential
  communication
confidentially
confiding
confine
confined
confinement
confines
confining
confirm
confirmation
confirmation dative
confirmation nominate
confiscate
confiscated
confiscating
confiscation
conflagration
conflict
confluence
conform
conformation
conformity
confound
confront
confrontation
confuse
confused
confusing
confusio

confusion
confusion of goods
congeal
congealed
congealing
congenial
congenially
congenital
congested
congestion
conglomeration
congratulate
congratulated
congratulating
congratulations
congratulatory
congregate
congregated
congregating
congregation
congregational
congress
congresses
congruent
congruity
congruous
conjectural
conjecture
conjectured
conjecturing
conjoin
conjugal
conjugate
conjugated
conjugating
conjugation
conjunct
conjunct and confident
conjunct and several
conjunct proof
conjunction
conjure

conjured
conjuring
connect
connected persons
connection
conned
conning
connivance
connive at
conniving at
connoisseur
connotation
conquer
conquered
conquering
conqueror
conquest
consanguinean
consanguinity
conscience
conscientious
conscientiousness
conscious
consciousness
conscript
conscription
consecutive
consecutively
consecutive
  sentences
consensus
consensus ad idem
consensus in idem
consensus tollit
  errorem
consent
consent judgement
consequence
consequent
consequential
consequently
conservation

conservation area
conservationist
conservative
conserve
conserved
conserving
consider
considerable
considerably
considerate
considerately
consideration
considered
considering
consign
consignment
consist
consistency
consistent
consistorial
consistorial action
consistory court
consolation
console
consoled
consolidate
consolidated
Consolidated Fund
consolidating
consolidation
Consolidation Act
consolidation of
  actions
consolidation of
  mortgages
consoling
consols
consonant
consort
consortium
conspicuous
conspiracies

conspiracy
conspiracy to defraud
conspirator
conspire
conspired
conspiring
constable
constabulary
constancy
constant
constat
constellation
consternation
constituencies
constituency
constituent
constitute
constituted
constituting
constitution
constitutional
constitutionally
constrain
constraint
constrict
construct
construction
constructive
constructive desertion
constructive dismissal
constructive fraud
constructively
constructive malice
constructive
  manslaughter
construe
consul
consulate
consult
consultant
consultation
consume

consumed
consumer
consumer credit
  agreement
consumer credit
  business
consumer credit
  register
consumer goods
consumer hire
  agreement
consumer protection
consumer safety
consumer trade
  practice
consuming
consummate
consummated
consummating
consummation
consumption
contact
contagious
contain
contained
container
containing
contaminate
contaminated
contaminating
contamination
contango
contemnor
contemplate
contemplated
contemplating
contemplation
contemporanea
  expositio
contemporary
contempt
contempt of court

contempt of statute
contemptible
contemptibly
contemptuous
contend
content
contented
contention
contentious
contentious business
contentious probate
  business
contentment
contents
contest
contestant
context
continent
continental
contingencies
contingency
contingent
contingent legacy
contingent remainder
continual
continually
continuance
continuation
continue
continued
continuing
continuity
continuous
continuous bail
continuous
  employment
continuously
contort
contortion
contra
contra bonos mores
contra proferentem

contraband
contraception
contraceptive
contract
contract by
  correspondence
contract for
  differences
contract for services
contract of
  employment
contract of record
contract of sale
contract of service
contract under seal
contracting out
contraction
contractor
contractual liability
contradict
contradiction
contradictory
contraption
contrary
contrast
contravene
contravened
contravening
contravention
contretemps
contribute
contributed
contributing
contribution
contributor
contributory
  negligence
contrite
contritely
contrition
contrivance
contrive

contrived
contriving
control
controlled
controlled drugs
controlled tenancy
controlled trust
controller
controlling
controlling director
controls
controversial
controversially
controversies
controversy
contumacious
contumacy
conundrum
conurbation
convalesce
convalesced
convalescence
convalescent
convalescing
convene
convened
convener
convenience
convenient
convening
convent
convention
conventional
conventionally
converge
converged
convergence
convergent
converging
conversant
conversation
conversational

conversationally
converse
conversed
conversing
conversion
conversion of title
convert
convertible
convex
convey
conveyance
conveyed
conveying
conveyor belt
convict
conviction
convince
convinced
convincing
convocation
convoy
convoyed
convoying
convulse
convulsed
convulsing
convulsion
convulsive
convulsively
cool
cooling-off period
coolly
coolness
coop up
cooped up
co-operate
co-operated
co-operating
co-operation
co-operative
co-operatively
cooping up

co-opt
co-opted
co-opting
co-ordinate
co-ordinated
co-ordinating
co-ordination
co-ownership of real
    property
cope
coped
copied
copies
coping
copious
copy
copying
copyright
coram
coram judice
cord
cordial
cordiality
cordially
cordite
cordon
cordon off
cordoned off
cordoning off
core
cored
co-respondent
coring
cornea
corner
cornered
cornering
corner-stone
corollaries
corollary
coronaries
coronary

coroner
corporal
corporal punishment
corporate
corporate body
corporate liability
corporate veil
corporation
corporation aggregate
corporation by
 prescription
corporation sole
corporation tax
corporeal
 hereditaments
corps
corpse
corpulence
corpulent
corpus delicti
corpuscle
correct
correction
corrective
correspond
correspondence
correspondent
corridor
corrigenda
corrigendum
corroborate
corroborated
corroborating
corroboration
corroborative
corrode
corroded
corroding
corrosion
corrosive
corrugated
corrupt

corruptible
corruption
cortège
cosh
coshes
cosmetic
cosmic
cosmonaut
cosmopolitan
cosset
cosseted
cosseting
cost
cost, insurance,
 freight (CIF)
costed
costing
costliness
costly
costs reserved
costume
coterie
cottage
couch
couchant
couches
cough
could
council
Council of Ministers
councillor
counsel
counselled
counselling
counsellor
count
count reckoning and
 payment
countenance
countenanced
countenancing
counter

counter action
counteract
counterclaim
countered
counterfeit
counterfeit notes
counterfeiting
counterfoil
countering
countermand
counter-offer
counterpane
counterpart
countersign
countess
countesses
counties
countless
countries
country
countryside
county
county council
county court
county court action
county court registrar
coup
couple
coupled
couplet
coupling
coupon
courage
courageous
courier
course
course of employment
coursing
court
Court of Appeal (CA)
Court of Arches
Court of Chivalry

Court of Criminal
  Appeal
Court of Ecclesiastical
  Causes Reserved
Court of Exchequer
Court of Faculties
court of first instance
Court of High
  Commission
Court of Justice of the
  European
  Communities
court of last resort
Court of Probate
Court of Protection
court of record
Court of Session
court of summary
  jurisdiction
Court of Tynwald
courteous
courtesy
courtier
courtly
court-martial
courtship
courts-martial
courtyard
cousin
cove
coven
covenant
cover
cover note
coverage
covered
covering
coverlet
covert
coverture
covet
coveted

coveting
covetous
covetousness
covey
coward
cowardice
cowardly
cowed
cower
cowered
cowering
coy
crack
cracker
crackle
crackled
crackling
craft
craftily
craftsman
crafty
cram
crammed
cramming
cramp
cramped
crane
crank
crannies
cranny
crash
crashes
crass
crate
crated
crater
crating
cravat
crave
craved
craving
crawl

craze
crazily
crazy
crease
creased
creasing
create
created
creating
creation
creative
creator
creature
crèche
credentials
credibility
credible
credibly
credit
credit card
credit limit
credit reference
  agency
credit sale
credit sale agreement
credit token
creditable
credited
crediting
creditor
creditor's petition
credulity
credulous
creed
creep
creeping
cremate
cremated
cremating
cremation
crematorium
creosote

crept
crescent
crestfallen
crevasse
crevice
crew
crib
cribbed
cribbing
cried
crier
cries
crime
crimen falsi
criminal
criminal appeal
criminal bankruptcy
  order
criminal damage
Criminal Injuries
  Compensation
  Board
Criminal Law Revision
  Committee
criminal libel
criminal lunatic
criminal negligence
criminal offence
criminally
cringe
cringed
cringing
cripple
crippled
crippling
crises
crisis
criteria
criterion
critic
critical
critically

criticism
criticize
criticized
criticizing
croak
croaky
crockery
croft
crofter
cronies
crony
crook
crooked
crookedness
croon
crooned
crooner
crooning
crop
cropped
cropper
cropping
croquet
cross
cross action
cross examination
cross-appeal
crossed
crosses
cross-examination
cross-examine
cross-examined
cross-examining
crossing
crossness
cross-offer
crossroads
cross-section
crouch
croup
croupier
crow

crowbar
crowd
crowded
crowed
crowing
crown
Crown Agent
Crown copyright
Crown Court
Crown interest
Crown land
Crown Office
Crown privilege
Crown property
Crown Prosecution
  Service
Crown servant
crucial
crucially
crucible
crucified
crucifix
crucifixes
crucifixion
crucify
crucifying
crude
crudely
crudeness
crudity
cruel
cruelly
cruelty
cruise
cruised
cruiser
cruising
crumb
crumble
crumbled
crumbling
crumbly

crumpet
crumple
crumpled
crumpling
crunch
crusade
crusader
crush
crust
crustacean
crusty
crutch
crutches
crux
cry
crying
crypt
cryptic
cryptically
crystal
crystalline
crystallization
crystallization of
  charge
crystallize
crystallized
crystallizing
cub
cube
cubic
cubicle
cuckoo
cucumber
cud
cuddle
cuddled
cuddling
cudgel
cue
cuff
cufflinks
cuisine

cujus est solum ejus
  est usque ad
  coelum et ad inferos
cul-de-sac
culinary
cull
culminate
culminated
culminating
culmination
culpa
culpable
culpable homicide
culprit
cult
cultivate
cultivated
cultivating
cultivation
culture
cultured
cum dividend
cum testamento
  annexo
cumbersome
cummerbund
cumulative
cumulative legacy
cumulo
cumulus
cunning
cup
cupboard
cupful
cupidity
cupola
cupped
cupping
cup-tie
cur
curable
curate

curator
curator ad litem
curator bonis
curb
curd
curdle
curdled
curdling
cure
cured
curfew
curia advisari vult (cur
  adv vult)
curing
curio
curiosities
curiosity
curious
curl
curlew
curling
curly
currant
currencies
currency
current
curricula
curricula vitae
curriculum
curriculum vitae
curriculums
curried
curries
curry
currying
curse
cursed
cursing
cursor
cursorily
cursory
curt

curtail
curtailed
curtailing
curtailment
curtain
curtain clauses
curtesy
curtilage
curtness
curtsey
curtseying
curtsied
curtsies
curtsy
curtsying
curvature
curve
curved
curving
cushion
cushioned
cushioning
cushy
custard
custodian
custodian trustee
custodianship
custody
custody officer
custody orders
custody record
custom
custom and contract
customarily
customary
customer
customs duties
cut
cute
cutely
cuteness
cuticle

cutlass
cutlasses
cutlery
cutlet
cutting
cut-up
cyanide
cycle
cycled
cyclical
cycling
cyclist
cyclone
cylinder
cylindrical
cylindrically
cynic
cynical
cynically
cynicism
cynosure
cy-près
cyst
cystitis
Czech

Dd

dab
dabbed
dabbing
dabble
dabbled
dabbling
dachshund
daft
dagger
dailies

daily
daintily
daintiness
dainty
dais
daises
daisy-wheel
dale
dalliance
dallied
dally
dallying
dam
damage
damage feasant
damaged
damages
damaging
dammed
damn
damnable
damnation
damned
damning
damnum
damnum absque
   injuria
damnum fatale
damnum sine injuria
damp
dampen
dampened
dampening
damper
dampness
dance
danced
dancer
dancing
dandruff
danger
dangerous

dangle
dangled
dangling
Danish
dank
dapper
dappled
dare
dared
daredevil
daring
dark
darken
darkened
darkening
darkness
darling
darn
dart
dartboard
dash
dashes
dashing
dastardly
data
database
date
dated
dating
datum
daub
daubed
daubing
daughter
daughter-in-law
daunt
dauntless
dawdle
dawdled
dawdling
dawn
dawn raid

day
day certain
day training centre
daydream
days of grace
daze
dazed
dazing
dazzle
dazzled
dazzling
de bene esse
de bonis asportatis
de bonis non
    administratis
de bonis propriis
de calumnia
de die in diem
de donis
    conditionalibus
de facto
de fideli
    administratione
    officii (de fideli)
de jure
de minimis non curat
    lex (de minimis)
de momento in
    momentum
de novo
de plano
de praxi
de presenti
de son tort
dead
dead rent
deaden
deadened
deadening
deadline
deadliness
deadly

deadness
dead's part
deaf
deafen
deafened
deafening
deafness
deal
dealer
dealing
dealt
Dean of Faculty
dearly
dearness
dearth
death
death duties
death penalty
deathly
debar
debarred
debarring
debase
debased
debasement
debasing
debatable
debate
debated
debating
debauched
debauchery
debenture
debenture stock
debenture trust deed
debilitate
debilitated
debilitating
debility
debit
debited
debiting

Dd

debitum fundi
debonair
débris
debt
debt-adjusting
debt-collecting
debtor
debtor-creditor
  agreement
debtor-creditor-
  supplier agreement
debtor's petition
decade
decadence
decadent
decanter
decapitate
decapitated
decapitating
decay
decayed
decaying
decease
deceased
deceit
deceitful
deceitfully
deceive
deceived
deceiver
deceiving
decelerate
decelerated
decelerating
December
decency
decent
deception
deceptive
deceptively
decern
decibel

decide
decided
decidedly
deciding
decimae
decimal
decimalization
decimalize
decimalized
decimalizing
decimate
decimated
decimating
decipher
deciphered
deciphering
decision
decisive
decisively
deck
declaim
declaimed
declaiming
declamation
declamatory
declaration
declaration against
  interest
declaration of
  intention
declarator
declarator of expiry of
  the legal
declaratory judgement
declare
declared
declaring
declinature
decline
declined
declining
decode

decoded
decoding
decompose
decomposed
decomposing
decomposition
decorous
decorum
decoy
decoyed
decoying
decrease
decreased
decreasing
decree
decree arbitral
decree conform
decree dative
decree nisi
decreed
decreeing
decrepit
decried
decry
decrying
dedicate
dedicated
dedicating
dedication
dedication and
  acceptance
dedication of way
dedimus
dedimus potestatem
deduce
deduced
deducing
deduct
deduction
deed
deed of arrangement
deed of conveyance

deed of gift
deed poll
deem
deemed
deeming
deep
deepen
deepened
deepening
deface
defaced
defacement
defacing
defamation
defamatory
defame
defamed
defaming
default
default notice
default summons
defaulter
defeasance
defeasible
defeat
defeated
defeating
defect
defection
defective
defectum sanguinis
defence
defenceless
defend
defendant
defender
defensible
defensive
defensively
defer
deference
deferential

deferentially
deferred
deferred debts
deferred sentence
deferred shares
deferring
defiance
defiant
deficiencies
deficiency
deficient
deficit
defied
defile
defiled
defilement
defiling
define
defined
defining
definite
definitely
definition
definitive
definitively
deflate
deflated
deflating
deflation
deflect
deflection
deforcement
deform
deformed
deformities
deformity
defraud
defray
defrayed
defraying
deft
defunct

defunct company
defy
defying
degenerate
degenerated
degenerating
degenerative
degradation
degrade
degraded
degrading
degree
dehors
dehydrate
dehydrated
dehydrating
dehydration
deign
deigned
deigning
dejected
dejection
del credere agent
delay
delayed
delaying
delectus personae
delegate
delegated
delegated legislation
delegating
delegation
delegatus non potest
    delegare
delete
deleted
deleterious
deleting
deletion
deliberate
deliberated
deliberately

deliberating
deliberation
delict
delight
delighted
delightful
delightfully
delinquency
delinquent
delirious
delirium
deliver
deliverable state
deliverance
delivered
deliveries
delivering
delivery
delude
deluded
deluding
deluge
deluged
deluging
delusion
delve
delved
delving
demand
demanding with
    menaces
demarcation
demarkation
demean
demeaned
demeaning
demeanour
demented
demesne
demise
demob
demobbed

demobbing
demobilization
demobilize
demobilized
demobilizing
democracies
democracy
democrat
democratic
democratically
demolish
demolition
demolition order
demonstrable
demonstrably
demonstrate
demonstrated
demonstrating
demonstration
demonstrative
demonstrative legacy
demonstrator
demoralize
demoralized
demoralizing
demote
demoted
demoting
demotion
demur
demure
demurely
demureness
demurrage
demurred
demurrer
demurring
den
denial
denied
denigrate
denigrated

denigrating
denizen
denomination
denominational
denominator
denote
denoted
denoting
dénouement
denounce
denounced
denouncing
dense
densely
denseness
densities
density
dent
denture
denudation
denude
denuded
denuding
denunciation
deny
denying
depart
department
departure
depend
dependable
dependant
dependence
dependent
dependent territory
depict
deplete
depleted
depleting
depletion
deplorable
deplorably

deplore
deplored
deploring
deploy
deployed
deploying
depone
deponent
depopulated
deport
deportation
deportation order
deportment
depose
deposed
deposing
deposit
Deposit Protection
  Board
deposit receipt
deposition
depositor
depositories
depository
depot
deprave
depraved
depravity
deprecate
deprecated
deprecating
depreciate
depreciated
depreciating
depredation
depress
depression
deprivation
deprivation of
  citizenship
deprive
deprived

depriving
deprogram
depth
deputation
deputies
deputize
deputized
deputizing
deputy
derail
derailed
derailing
derailment
deranged
derangement
derelict
dereliction
deride
derided
deriding
derision
derisive
derisively
derivation
derivative
derivative action
derivative deed
derivative trust
derive
derived
deriving
dermatitis
dermatologist
dermatology
derogate
derogatorily
derogatory
derrick
descend
descendant
descended
descendent

descending
descent
describe
described
describing
description
descriptive
desecrate
desecrated
desecrating
desecration
desert
desert the diet
deserter
desertion
deserve
deserved
deservedly
deserving
design
designate
designated
designating
designation
designed
designing
desirability
desirable
desirably
desire
desired
desiring
desirous
desist
desk
desolate
desolated
desolation
despair
despaired
despairing
despatch

despatches
desperado
desperadoes
desperados
desperate
desperately
desperation
despicable
despicably
despise
despised
despising
despite
despoil
despoiled
despoiling
despoliation
despondency
despondent
despot
despotic
despotically
despotism
destination
destination over
destined
destiny
destitute
destroy
destroyed
destroyer
destroying
destructible
destruction
destructive
desultorily
desultory
detach
detachable
detached
detaching
detachment

detail
detailed
detailing
detain
detained
detaining
detect
detection
detective
détente
detention
detention centre
deter
deteriorate
deteriorated
deteriorating
deterioration
determinable fee
determinable interest
determination
determine
determined
determining
deterred
deterrent
deterring
detest
detestable
detestably
detestation
detonate
detonated
detonating
detonator
detour
detract
detraction
detriment
detrimental
devaluation
devastate
devastated

devastating
devastation
devastavit
develop
developed
developer
developing
development
development land
deviate
deviated
deviating
deviation
device
devil
devilish
devilling
devilry
devious
devise
devised
devisee
devising
devisor
devoid
devolution
devolve
devolved
devolving
devote
devoted
devotee
devoting
devotion
devour
devout
devoutness
Dewali
dexterity
dexterous
dextrous
diabetes

diabetic
diabolic
diabolical
diabolically
diagnose
diagnosed
diagnosing
diagnosis
diagnostic
diagonal
diagonally
diagram
diagrammatic
dial
dialect
dialectal
dialled
dialling
dialogue
diameter
diametric
diametrically
diamond
diaphragm
diaries
diarrhoea
diary
diatribe
dice
Dictaphone®
dictate
dictated
dictating
dictation
dictator
dictatorial
dictatorially
diction
dictionaries
dictionary
dictum
did

die
died
dies cedit
dies dominicus non
    est juridicus
dies non
dies venit
diesel
diet
differ
differed
difference
different
differentiate
differentiated
differentiating
differentiation
differing
difficult
difficulties
difficulty
diffidence
diffident
diffuse
digest
digestible
digestion
digestive
digit
digital
digitalis
dignified
dignitaries
dignitary
dignity
digress
digression
dilapidated
dilapidation
dilatation
dilate
dilated

dilating
dilatory
dilemma
diligence
diligent
dilute
diluted
diluting
dilution
dim
dimension
dimensional
diminish
diminished
    responsibility
diminution
diminutive
dimmed
dimming
dimness
din
dinned
dinning
dint
diocesan
diocese
dip
diphtheria
diphthong
diploma
diplomacy
diplomat
diplomatic
diplomatic privilege
diplomatically
dipped
dipping
dire
direct
direct evidence
direct examination
directed

directing
direction
directive
directly
directness
director
Director General of
  Fair Trading
  (DGFT)
Director of Public
  Prosecutions (DPP)
directories
directors' report
directory
dirt
dirtied
dirtily
dirtiness
dirty
dirtying
disabilities
disability
disable
disabled
disabled person
disablement
disabling
disabling statute
disabuse
disabused
disabusing
disadvantage
disadvantaged
disadvantageous
disaffected
disagree
disagreeable
disagreeably
disagreed
disagreeing
disagreement
disallow

disappear
disappearance
disappeared
disappearing
disappoint
disappointed
disappointment
disapproval
disapprove
disapproved
disapproving
disarm
disarming
disarrange
disarranged
disarrangement
disarranging
disarray
disaster
disastrous
disavowal
disbar
disbelief
disbelieve
disbelieved
disbelieving
disburse
discard
discern
discernible
discernibly
discerning
discernment
discharge
discharged
discharging
disciplinarian
disciplinary
disciplinary
  procedures
discipline
disclaim

disclaimed
disclaimer
disclose
disclosed
disclosing
disclosure
disclosure of
  documents
discoloration
discolour
discolouration
discoloured
discolouring
discomfiture
discomfort
disconcert
disconnect
disconnection
disconsolate
disconsolately
discontent
discontented
discontentment
discontinuance
discontinue
discontinued
discontinuing
discord
discordant
discount
discourage
discouraged
discouragement
discouraging
discourse
discoursed
discoursing
discourteous
discover
discovered
discoverer
discoveries

discovering
discovery
discovery and
inspection of
documents
discredit
discreditable
discredited
discrediting
discreet
discrepancies
discrepancy
discrete
discretion
discretionary trust
discriminate
discriminated
discriminating
discrimination
discuss
discussion
disdain
disdained
disdainful
disdainfully
disdaining
disease
disease of the mind
diseased
disengage
disengaged
disengaging
disentailing assurance
disentailing deed
disentailment
disentangle
disentangled
disentangling
disfavour
disfigure
disfigured
disfigurement

disfiguring
disfranchise
disgrace
disgraced
disgraceful
disgracefully
disgracing
disgruntled
disguise
disguised
disguising
disgust
disgusted
dishearten
disheartened
disheartening
disherison
dishevelled
dishonest
dishonest
appropriation
dishonesty
dishonour
dishonour of bill
dishonourable
dishonourably
disillusion
disillusioned
disillusioning
disillusionment
disinclined
disinfect
disinfectant
disinherit
disinherited
disinheriting
disintegrate
disintegrated
disintegrating
disintegration
disinterested
disjointed

dislike
disliked
disliking
dislocate
dislocated
dislocating
dislocation
dislodge
dislodged
dislodging
disloyal
disloyally
disloyalty
dismal
dismally
dismantle
dismantled
dismantling
dismay
dismayed
dismaying
dismember
dismembered
dismembering
dismemberment
dismiss
dismiss from
employment
dismissal
dismissal statement
dismount
disobedience
disobedient
disobey
disobeyed
disobeying
disobliging
disorder
disordered
disorderliness
disorderly
disorderly house

Dd

disown
disparage
disparaged
disparagement
disparagement of
   goods
disparaging
disparities
disparity
dispassionate
dispassionately
dispatch
dispatches
dispel
dispelled
dispelling
dispensable
dispensaries
dispensary
dispensation
dispense
dispense with service
dispensed
dispenser
dispensing
dispersal
disperse
dispersed
dispersing
dispirited
displace
displaced
displacement
displacing
display
displayed
displaying
displease
displeased
displeasing
displeasure
dispone

disposable
disposal
dispose
disposed
disposing
disposition
dispositive clause
dispossess
disproportionate
disproportionately
disprove
disputable
disputation
dispute
disputed
disputing
disqualification
disqualification order
disqualified
disqualify
disqualifying
disquiet
disquieting
disregard
disrepair
disreputable
disreputably
disrepute
disrespect
disrespectful
disrespectfully
disrupt
disruption
disruptive
diss
dissatisfaction
dissatisfied
dissatisfy
dissatisfying
dissect
disseisin
dissemble

dissembled
dissembling
disseminate
disseminated
disseminating
dissemination
dissension
dissent
dissented
dissenter
dissentiente
dissenting
dissertation
disservice
dissimilar
dissimilarities
dissimilarity
dissimulate
dissimulated
dissimulating
dissipate
dissipated
dissipating
dissipation
dissociate
dissociated
dissociating
dissociation
dissolute
dissolution
dissolution of
   marriage
dissolve
dissolved
dissolving
dissuade
dissuaded
dissuading
distance
distant
distaste
distasteful

distastefully
distend
distension
distil
distillation
distilled
distilling
distinct
distinction
distinctive
distinguish
distinguished
distort
distortion
distract
distraction
distrain
distraint
distraught
distress
distress damage
  feasant
distribute
distributed
distributing
distribution
distributive justice
district
district council
district court
district registrar
district registry
distrust
distrustful
distrustfully
disturb
disturbance
disuse
disused
ditto
Divali
diverge

diverged
divergence
divergent
diverging
diverse
diversification
diversified
diversify
diversifying
diversion
diversity
divert
divest
divide
divided
dividend
dividing
divination
divine
Divine Right of Kings
divined
divining
divisibility
divisible
divisible contract
division
divisional
Divisional Court (DC)
Divisions of the High
  Court
divisor
divorce
divorce by mutual
  consent
divorced
divorcee
divorcing
divulge
divulged
divulging
Diwali
dizziness

dizzy
do
docile
docilely
docility
dock
dock statement
docker
docket
docquet (docket)
doctor
doctored
doctoring
doctrinal
doctrine
document
document exchange
document of debt
documentaries
documentary
documentary
  evidence
dodge
dodged
dodging
doer
does
dogged
doggedly
dogma
dogmatic
dogmatically
doing
dole
dole out
doled out
doleful
dolefully
dolefulness
doli capax
doli incapax
doling out

dollar
dolus
domain
dome
Domesday Book
domestic
domestic animal
domestic arbitration
domestic court
domestic premises
domestic tribunal
domestic violence
domestically
domesticated
domesticity
domicile
domicile of choice
domicile of
  dependence
domicile of origin
domiciled
dominance
dominant
dominant tenement
dominate
dominated
dominating
domination
domineer
domineered
domineering
dominion
dominium
dominium directum
dominium utile
dominus lites
domitae naturae
domus sua cuique est
  tutissimum refugium
don
donate
donated

donating
donatio mortis causa
donation
donation inter vivos
donation mortis causa
donatory
done
donned
donning
donor
don't
doom
doomed
door
doorway
dope
doped
doping
dormant
dormant company
dormant partner
dormitories
dormitory
dose
dosed
dosing
doss down
dossier
dotard
dote on
doted on
doting on
double
double distress
double insurance
double jeopardy
double portions
double probate
double renvoi
doubled
double-entry
doubling

doubly
doubt
doubted
doubtful
doubtfully
doubting
doubtless
dovetail
dovetailed
dovetailing
dowdily
dowdy
Dow-Jones
down
downfall
downstairs
downtrodden
downwards
dowries
dowry
doze
dozed
dozen
dozing
drab
draft
drag
dragged
dragging
dragooned
dragooning
drain
drainage
drama
dramatic
dramatically
dramatist
dramatization
dramatize
dramatized
dramatizing
drank

drape
draped
draping
drastic
drastically
draught
draughtsman
draughty
draw
drawee
drawer
drawing
drawn
dread
dreadful
dreadfully
dreadfulness
dream
dreamed
dreamily
dreaming
dreamt
dreamy
drearily
dreary
dredge
dredged
dredger
dredging
dregs
drench
dress
dressed
dresser
dresses
dressing
drew
dried
drift
drill
drily
drink

drinking
drip
dripped
dripping
drive
drivel
drivelled
drivelling
driven
driver
driving
driving licence
droll
drone
droned
droning
droop
drooped
drooping
drop
dropped
dropping
dross
drove
drove road
drown
drowsily
drowsy
drudge
drudged
drudgery
drudging
drug
drug trafficking
drugged
drugging
druggist
drunk
drunkard
drunken
drunkenness
dry

drying
dryly
dual
dub
dubbed
dubbing
dubiety
dubious
dubitante
duces tecum
duct
dudgeon
due
due care
due diligence
due process of law
dug
dug-out
duke
dukedom
dulcet
dull
dullness
dully
duly
dum bene se gesserit
dum casta vixerit
dum sola
dumb
dumbfound
dumbly
dumbness
dump
dungeon
dupe
duped
duping
duplicate
duplicated
duplicating
duplication
duplicity

durable
durably
durante absentia
durante minore aetate
durante viduitate
duration
duress
duress of goods
duress per minas
during
during Her Majesty's
  pleasure
Dutch
Dutch auction
dutiable
duties
dutiful
dutifully
duty
duty of care
duty solicitor
dwell
dwelled
dwelling
dwelt
dwindle
dwindled
dwindling
dying
dying declaration
dynamic
dynamically
dynamite
dynamo
dysentery
dyspepsia
dyspeptic

Ee

each
eager
eagerness
ear
eardrum
earl
earlier
earliest
earliness
early
earmark
earn
earned income
earnest
earnings
earth
ease
eased
easement
easement of light
easier
easiest
easily
easing
east
Easter
easterly
eastern
eastward
eastwards
easy
eaves
eavesdrop
eavesdropped
eavesdropping
ebb
ebullience
ebullient

eccentric
eccentricities
eccentricity
ecclesiastic
ecclesiastical
ecclesiastical court
echo
echoes
eclipse
eclipsed
eclipsing
ecological
ecologically
ecologist
ecology
economic
economic duress
economical
economically
economics
economies
economist
economize
economized
economizing
economy
eczema
edge
edged
edgeways
edging
edible
edict
edictal citation
edification
edifice
edified
edify
edifying
Edinburgh Gazette
edit
edited

emptiness
empty
emptying
emulate
emulated
emulating
emulation
emulsion
en masse
en ventre sa mère
enable
enabled
enabling
enabling statute
enact
enactment
enclose
enclosed
enclosing
enclosure
encompass
encounter
encountered
encountering
encourage
encouraged
encouragement
encouraging
encroach
encroachment
encumbrance
encumbrancer
encyclopaedia
encyclopaedic
encyclopedia
encyclopedic
end
endanger
endangered
endangering
endeavour
endemic

ending
endorse
endorsed
endorsee
endorsement
endorsement in blank
endorsing
endow
endowment
endurance
endure
endured
enduring
enemies
enemy
energetic
energetically
energies
energy
enervate
enervated
enervating
enforce
enforced
enforcement
enforcing
enfranchise
enfranchisement of
  tenancy
engage
engage
engagement
engaging
engine
engineer
engineered
engineering
English
engross
engrossment
enhance
enhanced

enhancing
enigma
enigmatic
enigmatically
enjoy
enjoyable
enjoyed
enjoying
enjoyment
enlarge
enlarged
enlargement
enlarging
enlighten
enlightened
enlightening
enlightenment
enlist
enliven
enlivened
enlivening
enmity
enorm lesion
enormity
enormous
enough
enprint
enquire
enquirer
enquiries
enquiring
enquiry
enrage
enraged
enraging
enrol
enroll
enrolled
enrolling
enrolment
ensemble
ensue

ensued
ensuing
ensure
ensured
ensuring
entail
entailed
entailed interest
entailing
entangle
entangled
entanglement
entangling
enter
enter appearance
enter judgement
entered
entering
enterprise
enterprise zones
enterprising
entertain
entertained
entertainer
entertaining
entertainment
enthuse
enthused
enthusiasm
enthusiast
enthusiastic
enthusiastically
enthusing
entice
enticed
enticement
enticing
entire
entire contract
entirely
entirety
entitle

entitled
entitling
entity
entrance
entrant
entrapment
entreat
entreated
entreaties
entreating
entreaty
entrenched
entrepot
entrepreneur
entries
entrust
entry
entry into possession
enumerate
enumerated
enumerating
enumeration
enunciate
enunciated
enunciating
enunciation
enure
envelop
envelope
enveloped
enveloping
enviable
enviably
envied
envious
environment
environmental
environmentalist
environmentally
envisage
envisaged
envisaging

envoy
envy
envying
enzyme
eodem die
epidemic
epiglottis
epilepsy
epileptic
episcopacy
episcopal
episcopalian
episode
episodic
epistle
epitaph
epithet
epitome
epitome of title
epitomize
epitomized
epitomizing
equable
equably
equal
Equal Opportunities
    Commission
equal pay
equality
equalize
equalized
equalizing
equalled
equalling
equally
equanimity
equate
equated
equating
equation
equidistant
equilateral

equilibrium
equip
equipment
equipollent
equipped
equipping
equitable
equitable easement
equitable estoppel
equitable lease
equitable lien
equitable waste
equitably
equity
equity security
equity share capital
equity's darling
equivalent
equivocal
equivocally
equivocate
equivocated
equivocating
equivocation
eradicate
eradicated
eradicating
eradication
erase
erased
eraser
erasing
erect
erection
erode
eroded
eroding
erosion
err
errand
errant
errata

erratic
erratically
erratum
erred
erring
erroneous
error
erudite
eruditely
erudition
escalate
escalated
escalating
escalation
escalator
escapade
escape
escaped
escaping
escort
escrow
Eskimo
Eskimos
esoteric
especial
especially
Esperanto
espionage
Esq
essay
essayist
essence
essential
essentially
essoin
establish
establishment
estate
estate agency
estate duty
esteem
esteemed

esteeming
estimate
estimated
estimating
estimation
esto
estoppel
estoppel by deed
estoppel by record
estoppel in pais
estovers
estranged
estreat
estuaries
estuary
et al
et alia
et seq
et sequentes paginae
  (et sec)
etc
ether
ethical
ethically
ethics
ethnic
etiquette
eulogies
eulogize
eulogized
eulogizing
eulogy
euphemism
euphemistic
euphemistically
European
European Court
European Court of
  Human Rights
European Community
  (EC)
European Parliament

Ee

euthanasia
evade
evaded
evading
evaluate
evaluated
evaluating
evaluation
evaporate
evaporated
evaporating
evaporation
evasion
evasive
evasively
even
evenness
event
eventful
eventfully
eventual
eventualities
eventuality
eventually
ever
every
everybody
everyone
everything
everywhere
evict
eviction
evidence
evidenced in writing
evident
evidently
evil
evilly
evince
evinced
evincing
evocative

evocatively
evoke
evoked
evoking
evolve
evolved
evolving
ex abundanti cautela
ex capitalization (xc)
ex contractu
ex debito justitiae
ex dividend (xd)
ex dolo malo non
    oritur actio
ex facie
ex gratia
ex hypothese
ex hypothesi
ex nudo pacto non
    oritur actio
ex officio
ex parte
ex post facto
ex proprio motu
ex relatione (ex rel)
ex rights (xr)
ex turpi causa non
    oritur actio
exact
exacting
exactness
exaggerate
exaggerated
exaggerating
exaggeration
examination
examination in chief
examine
examined
examiner
examining
examining justice

example
exasperate
exasperated
exasperating
exasperation
excambion
excavate
excavated
excavating
excavation
excavator
exceed
exceedingly
excel
excelled
excellence
excellency
excellent
excelling
except
excepted perils
excepting
exception
exceptional
exceptionally
excerpt
excess
excesses
excessive
excessive
    appointment
excessively
exchange
exchange of contracts
exchanged
exchanging
exchequer
Exchequer, Court of
excise
excised
excising
excision

excitable
excitably
excite
excited
excitement
exciting
exclaim
exclaimed
exclaiming
exclamation
exclamatory
exclude
excluded
excluding
exclusion
exclusive
exclusively
excommunicate
excommunication
excrement
excrescence
excrete
excreted
excreting
excruciating
excursion
excusable homicide
excuse
excused
excusing
exeat
execrable
execrably
execute
executed
executing
execution
executioner
executive
executive warrant
executor
executor creditor

executor dative
executor de son tort
executor nominate
executor-dative
executor-nominate
executory
exemplary
exemplary damages
exemplified
exemplify
exemplifying
exempt
exemption
exercise
exercised
exercising
exert
exertion
exhaust
exhausted
exhausting
exhaustion
exhaustive
exhibit
exhibited
exhibiting
exhibition
exhibitionism
exhibitionist
exhibitor
exhilarate
exhilarated
exhilarating
exhort
exhortation
exhumation
exhume
exhumed
exhuming
exigencies
exigency
exigent

exile
exiled
exiling
exist
existence
exit
exited
exiting
exodus
exoduses
exoner
exonerate
exonerated
exoneration
exorbitance
exorbitant
expand
expanse
expansion
expansive
expatiate
expatiated
expatiating
expatriate
expatriation
expect
expectancy
expectant
expectant heir
expectation
expected
expecting
expede
expedience
expediency
expedient
expedite
expedited
expediting
expedition
expeditious
expel

expelled
expelling
expend
expenditure
expense
expensive
expensively
experience
experienced
experiencing
experiment
experimental
experimentally
expert
expert opinion
expertise
expiate
expiated
expiating
expire
expired
expiring
expiry
explain
explained
explaining
explanation
explanatory
expletive
explicable
explicably
explicit
explode
exploded
exploding
exploit
exploitation
exploited
exploiting
exploration
explore
explored

explorer
exploring
explosion
explosive
exponent
export
exportation
exporter
expose
exposed
exposing
exposition
exposure
expound
express
express term
express trust
expressio unius
    personae vel rei est
    exclusio alterius
expression
expressive
expressively
expressum facit
    cessare tacitum
expropriate
expropriated
expropriating
expropriation
expulsion
expurgate
expurgated
expurgating
exquisite
exquisitely
extant
extempore
extemporize
extemporized
extemporizing
extend
extension

extensive
extensively
extent
extenuate
extenuated
extenuating
extenuation
exterior
exterminate
exterminated
exterminating
extermination
external
externally
extinct
extinction
extinguish
extinguished
extinguisher
extinguishment
extol
extolled
extolling
extort
extortion
extortionate
extortionately
extra
extract
extraction
extradite
extradited
extraditing
extradition
extra-judicial
extraneous
extraordinarily
extraordinary
extraordinary general
    meeting (EGM)
extra-territoriality
extravagance

extravagant
extravert
extreme
extremely
extremist
extremities
extremity
extricate
extricated
extricating
extrinsic
extrinsic evidence
extrovert
exude
exuded
exuding
eye
eye witness
eyebrow
eyed
eyeing
eyelash
eyelid

Ff

fabric
fabricate
fabricated
fabricating
fabrication
façade
face
faced
facet
facetious
facetiousness
facial

facially
facile
facilely
facilitate
facilitated
facilitating
facilities
facility
facility and
    circumvention
facing
facsimile
fact
faction
factious
factor
factories
factoring
factory
factotum
factum probandum
factum probans
faculties
faculty
Faculty of Advocates
fade
faded
fading
faeces
faggot
Fahrenheit
fail
failed
failing
failure
failure to appear
failure to make
    discovery
faint
faintness
fair
fair comment

fair dismissal
fair rent
fair wear and tear
fairness
fait accompli
faith
faithful
faithfully
faithfulness
faithless
faithlessness
fake
faked
faking
fall
fallacies
fallacious
fallacy
fallen
fallibility
fallible
falling
fallow
falsa demonstratio
falsa demonstratio
    non nocet cum de
    corpore constat
false
false plea
false pretence
falsehood
falsehood, fraud and
    wilful imposition
falsely
falseness
falsification
falsified
falsify
falsifying
fame
familiar
familiarity

familiarize
familiarized
familiarizing
families
family
Family Division
famous
fanatic
fanatical
fanatically
fanciful
fantasies
fantasy
far
farce
farcical
fare
fared
farewell
faring
farm
farmer
farming
farrow
farther
farthest
fascinate
fascinated
fascinating
fascination
fashion
fashionable
fashionably
fashioned
fashioning
fast
fasten
fastened
fastening
fastidious
fastness
fat

fatal
fatalities
fatality
fatally
fate
fated
fateful
fatefully
father
father-in-law
fathom
fathomed
fathoming
fatigue
fatter
fattest
fatuous
fault
faultless
faulty
faux pas
favour
favourable
favourably
favoured
favouring
favourite
favouritism
fax machine
feal and divot
fealty
fear
fearful
fearfully
fearless
fearlessly
feasibility
feasible
feasibly
feat
feature
featured

featuring
February
fed
federal
federated
federation
fee
fee farm rent
fee fund
fee simple absolute in
    possession
fee simple conditional
fee tail
feeble
feebleness
feebly
feed
feeding
feel
feeling
feet
feign
feigned
feigning
fell
felled
felling
fellow
fellowship
felon
felonies
felony
felt
female
feme covert
feme sole
feminine
femininely
femininity
feminism
feminist
femur

fence
fenced
fencing
fend
fender
feodum
ferocious
ferocity
fertile
fertility
fertilization
fertilize
fertilized
fertilizer
fertilizing
fetch
fetid
fetish
fetishes
feu
feuar
feud
feudal
feudalism
feuduty
fever
fevered
feverish
few
fiancé
fiancée
fiar
fiat
fiat justitia, ruat
  coelum
fiat ut petitur
fibre
fibreglass
fibrous
fickle
fickleness
fiction

fictitious
fidelity
fiduciary
fief
field
field-marshal
fiend
fiendish
fierce
fiercely
fierceness
fieri facias (fi fa)
fieri feci
fiery
fifteen
fifteenth
fifth
fiftieth
fifty
fight
fighter
fighting
figment
figurative
figuratively
figure
figured
figurehead
filament
file
filed
filial
filiation
filing
filius nullius
fill
filled
filler
filling
film
Filofax®
filter

filtered
filtering
filth
filthy
final
final interlocutor
finality
finalization
finalize
finalized
finalizing
finally
finance
financed
financial
financial provision
financial services
financial year
financially
financier
financing
find
finding
fine
fined
finger
fingered
fingering
fingerprint
fining
finish
finished
finite
Finnish
fire
firearm
fired
fire-raising
firing
firm
firmness
first

first aid
first instance
First Lord of the
  Treasury
first offender
firstly
firth
fiscal
fishery
fission
fissure
fist
fisticuffs
fit
fitful
fitfully
fitness
fitted
fitted accounts
fitter
fittest
fitting
fittings
five
fix
fixed charge
fixedly
fixture
fixtures and fittings
flabbergasted
flabbiness
flabby
flaccid
flag
flagged
flagging
flagrancy
flagrant
flagrante delicto
flail
flailed
flailing

flak
flamboyance
flamboyant
flame
flamed
flaming
flammable
flap
flapped
flapping
flash
flashes
flashily
flashy
flask
flat
flatness
flatten
flattened
flattening
flatter
flattered
flattering
flattery
flattest
flaunt
flavour
flavoured
flavouring
flaw
flawed
flawless
fled
flee
fleeing
flesh
flew
flex
flexibility
flexible
flexitime
flick

flicker
flickered
flickering
flight
flinch
fling
flinging
flippancy
flippant
flirt
flirtation
flirtatious
flit
flitted
flitting
float
floated
floating
floating charge
flood
flooded
flooding
floor
floored
flooring
florid
flotation
flotsam
flounder
floundered
floundering
flourish
flourished
flourishes
flourishing
flout
flouted
flouting
flow
flowed
flowered
flowering

flowery
flowing
flown
flu
fluctuate
fluctuated
fluctuating
fluctuation
fluency
fluent
fluid
fluke
flung
fluoridate
fluoridation
fluoride
fluoridize
fluoridized
fluoridizing
flux
fly
flyover
fob
fob off
fobbed off
fobbing off
foci
focus
focused
focuses
focusing
focussed
focussing
foetid
foetus
fog
foggy
foil
foiled
foiling
foist
fold

folder
foliage
follow
followed
follower
following
foment
fond
fondle
fondled
fondling
fondness
font
food
fool
fooled
foolhardy
fooling
foolish
foolishness
foolproof
foolscap
foot
footpath
footprint
footstep
footwear
for
for hire or reward
forage
foraged
foraging
foray
forbade
forbear
forbearance
forbearing
forbid
forbidden
forbidding
forbore
force

force and fear
force majeure
forced
forceful
forcefully
forceps
forcible
forcibly
forcing
fore
forearm
foreboding
forecast
forecasting
foreclose
foreclosure
forefather
forefinger
forefront
foregone
foreground
forehand rent
forehead
foreign
foreigner
foreleg
forelock
foreman
foremen
foremost
forensic
forerunner
foresaw
foresee
foreseeing
foreseen
foreshore
foresight
forest
forestall
forestalled
forestalling

forester
forestry
foretaste
foretell
foretelling
forethought
foretold
forewarn
forewoman
forewomen
foreword
forfeit
forfeited
forfeiting
forfeiture
forgave
forge
forged
forgeries
forgery
forget
forgetful
forgetfully
forgetfulness
forgetting
forging
forgive
forgiven
forgiveness
forgiving
forgo
forgoing
forgone
forgot
forgotten
forisfamiliation
form
formal
formalities
formality
formally
format

formation
former
formerly
formidable
formidably
formula
formulae
formulas
formulate
formulated
formulating
formulation
forsake
forsaken
forsaking
forsook
forswear
forswearing
forswore
forsworn
forth
forthcoming
forthright
forthwith
fortieth
fortitude
fortnight
fortnightly
Fortran
fortuitous
fortunate
fortunately
fortune
forty
forum
forum non conveniens
forum rei
forward
forwards
forwent
foster
foster-child

fostered
fostering
foster-parent
fought
found
foundation
founded
founder
foundered
foundering
founding
foundries
foundry
four
fourteen
fourteenth
fourth
fracas
fraction
fractional
fractionally
fractious
fracture
fractured
fracturing
fragile
fragment
fragmentary
frail
frailties
frailty
frame
framed
framework
framing
franc
franchise
frank
frantic
frantically
fraternal
fraternity

fraternization
fraternize
fraternized
fraternizing
fraud
fraud on a power
fraudulent
fraudulent medium
fraudulent
   misrepresentation
fraudulent preference
fraudulent trading
fraught
freak
freakish
free
free on board (FOB)
freedom
freedom of contract
freehold
freelance
freely
freight
freighter
freightliner
French
frenetic
frenetically
frenzied
frenzy
frequencies
frequency
frequent
frequenting
fresh
friction
Friday
friend
friendliness
friendly
friendly society
friendship

frigate
fright
frighten
frightened
frightening
frightful
frightfully
frigid
frigidity
fringe
fringed
fringing
fritter
frittered
frittering
frivolities
frivolity
frivolous
frivolous action
fro
frogman
frogmen
from
front
frontage
frontier
frontispiece
fructus
fructus industriales
frugal
frugality
frugally
fruitful
fruitfully
fruition
fruitless
fruitlessly
frustate
frustrate
frustrated
frustrating
frustration

fuel
fugitive
fulcra
fulcrum
fulcrums
fulfil
fulfilled
fulfilling
fulfilment
full
full bench
fullness
fully
fulminate
fulminated
fulminating
fulsome
fulsomely
fume
fumed
fumigate
fumigated
fumigating
fumigation
fuming
function
functional
functionally
functioned
functioning
functus officio
fund
fund in medio
fundamental
fundamentally
funeral
funereal
fungi
fungible
fungus
funguses
funnel

furbish
furious
furlong
furnace
furnish
furnishings
furniture
furore
furrow
furth of
furthcoming
further
furthered
furthering
furthermore
furthest
furtive
furtively
fury
fuse
fused
fuselage
fusing
fusion
fuss
fussed
fussing
futile
futilely
futility
future

Gg

gable
gadget
Gaelic
gag

gage
gagged
gagging
gain
gained
gaining
gait
gall
gallbladder
galleries
gallery
galling
gallon
gallows
Gallup poll
galvanize
galvanized
galvanizing
gambit
gamble
gambled
gambling
game
gamekeeper
gaming
gamut
gang
gang up
ganged up
ganging up
gangrene
gangrenous
gangster
gangway
gantries
gantry
gaol
gaoler
gap
gape
gaped
gaping

garage
garaged
garaging
garbled
gargantuan
garish
garment
garnishee
garret
garrison
garrisoned
garrisoning
garrotte
garrotted
garrotting
garrulity
garrulous
gas
gaseous
gases
gash
gashes
gasometer
gassed
gassing
gastric
gate
gatecrash
gatecrasher
gather
gathered
gathering
gauche
gaudily
gaudiness
gaudy
gauge
gauged
gauging
gaunt
gauntlet
gave

gazette
gazetted
gazetteer
gazetting
gazump
gazunder
gear
gear to
geared to
gearing to
gem
gender
gene
genealogical
genealogies
genealogist
genealogy
genera
general
general counts
general disposition
general equitable
  charge
general intent
general legacy
general lien
general service
generalia specialibus
  non derogant
generalia verba sunt
  generaliter
  intelligenda
generalibus specialia
  derogant
generalization
generalize
generalized
generalizing
generally
generate
generated
generating

generation
generator
generosity
generous
genesis
genetic
genetically
genetics
genial
genially
genius
geniuses
genocide
gentile
gentleman
gentlemanly
gentlemen
gentry
genuine
genuinely
genuineness
genus
geographical
geographically
geography
geological
geologically
geologist
geology
geometric
geometrically
geometry
germ
German
germane
germinate
germinated
germinating
germination
gestate
gestation
gesticulate

gesticulated
gesticulating
gesticulation
gesture
gestured
gesturing
get
getting
ghetto
ghoul
ghoulish
giant
gibber
gibbered
gibbering
gibberish
gibbet
gibe
gibed
gibing
giddiness
giddy
gift
gift over
gifted
gigantic
gild
gill
gillie
gilt
gilt-edged
gimcrack
gimlet
gimmick
gingerly
gipsies
gipsy
gird
girder
girdle
girl
girlhood

girlish
giro
girth
gist
give
given
giving
glad
gladden
gladdened
gladdening
gladness
glamorous
glamour
glance
glanced
glancing
gland
glandular
glare
glared
glaring
glass
glasses
glassily
glassy
glaze
glazed
glazier
glazing
gleam
gleamed
gleaming
glean
gleaned
gleaning
glebe
glen
glib
glibness
glide
glided

glider
gliding
glimmer
glimmered
glimmering
glimpse
glimpsed
glimpsing
gloat
global
globally
globe
globular
globule
gloss
glossaries
glossary
glosses
glower
glowered
glowering
glucose
glue
glued
gluey
gluing
glut
glutted
glutting
glutton
gluttonous
gluttony
glycerine
gnaw
go
goad
go-ahead
goal
god
goddess
goddesses
godfather

godliness
godly
godmother
going
goitre
gold
golden
golden handcuffs
golden parachute
golden rule
gone
good
good faith
goodbye
good-day
goodly
goodness
goods
goodwill
gory
go-slow
gospel
gossip
gossiped
gossiping
got
gouge
gouged
gouging
gourmet
gout
govern
governed
governess
governesses
governing
government
governor
gown
grab
grabbed
grabbing

gracious
graciousness
gradation
grade
graded
gradient
grading
gradual
gradually
gradualness
graduate
graduated
graduating
graduation
graffiti
graft
Grail
grain
gram
grammar
grammatical
grammatically
gramme
gramophone
granaries
granary
grand
grand jury
grandchild
grandchildren
grand-daughter
grandeur
grandfather
grandiloquent
grandiose
grandmother
grandson
grandstand
granite
grant
grant-in-aid
granular

granule
graph
graphic
graphite
grapple
grappled
grappling
grasp
grassum
grate
grateful
gratefully
gratification
gratified
gratify
gratifying
grating
gratis
gratitude
gratuities
gratuitous
gratuity
grave
gravel
gravely
graveyard
gravitate
gravitated
gravitating
gravitation
gravity
gray
Gray's Inn
graze
grazed
grazing
grease
greased
greasing
greasy
great
greatness

greed
greedily
greediness
greedy
Greek
green
greenery
greenmail
greet
greeted
greeting
gregarious
grenade
grew
grey
grid
grief
grievance
grieve
grieved
grieving
grievous
grievous bodily harm
   (GBH)
grille
grim
grimace
grimaced
grimacing
grime
grimness
grin
grind
grinding
grinned
grinning
grip
gripe
griped
griping
gripped
gripping

grisly
grit
gritted
gritting
groat
groin
groove
gross
gross value
grossly
grossness
grotesque
grotesquely
grotesqueness
ground
ground annual
ground rent
grounded
grounding
groundless
groundwork
group
grouped
grouping
grove
grow
growing
grown
growth
grudge
grudged
grudging
gruelling
gruesome
guarantee
guaranteed
guaranteeing
guarantor
guard
guardian
guardian ad litem
guardianship

guerrilla
guess
guessed
guesses
guessing
guest
guidance
guide
guided
guiding
guild
guile
guileless
guilt
guiltily
guilty
guinea
guise
gulf
gull
gullet
gullible
gullibly
gumption
gun
gunfire
gunned
gunnel
gunning
gunpowder
gunwale
gusto
gutter
guttural
gutturally
gypsies
gypsy
gyrate
gyrated
gyrating
gyratory

Hh

habeas corpus
habendum
habile
habili modo
habit
habit and repute
habitable
habitat
habitation
habitual
habitually
habituate
habituated
habituating
had
Hades
haemoglobin
haemorrhage
haemorrhaged
haemorrhaging
haereditas iacens
Hague Rules
hair
halcyon
hale
half
halfpennies
halfpenny
hallmark
hallow
hallucinate
hallucinated
hallucinating
hallucination
halt
halter
halting
halve

halved
halves
halving
hamesucken
hamlet
hammer
hammered
hammering
hamstring
hamstringing
hamstrung
hand
handcuffs
handful
handicap
handicapped
handle
handled
handling
handwriting
hang
hanged
hanging
Hansard
haphazard
hapless
happen
happened
happening
happier
happiest
happily
happiness
happy
harangue
harangued
haranguing
harass
harassed
harassing
harassment
harbinger

harbour
harboured
harbouring
hard
harden
hardened
hardening
hardily
hardiness
hardly
hardness
hardship
hardy
harm
harmful
harmfully
harmless
harmonisation
harmonize
harness
harnesses
harried
harrier
harrow
harrowing
harry
harrying
harsh
harshness
harvest
harvester
hassock
haste
hasten
hastened
hastening
hastily
hasty
hat
hatch
hatcheries
hatchery

hatches
hatchet
hatchway
hate
hated
hateful
hatefully
hating
hatred
haul
haulage
hauled
hauling
haunch
haunches
have
haven
haver
having
hay bote
hazard
hazardous
he
head
head lease
head note
headed
heading
headings
headlight
headline
headmaster
headmistress
headmistresses
headquarters
headway
heal
healed
healing
health
Health Service
    Commissioner

Hh

healthily
healthy
heap
heaped
heaping
hear
heard
hearing
hearsay
hearsay evidence
hearse
heart
hearth
heartless
heat
heated
heating
heave
heave to
heaved
heavier
heaviest
heavily
heaviness
heaving
heaving to
heavy
Hebrew
heckle
heckled
heckler
heckling
hectare
hector
hectored
hectoring
he'd
hedge
hedged
hedgerow
hedging
heed

heedless
height
heighten
heightened
heightening
heinous
heinousness
heir
heir apparent
heir presumptive
heiress
heiresses
heirloom
heirs in mobilibus
heirs of the body
held
helicopter
helium
he'll
helm
helmet
helmsman
help
helpful
helpfully
helpfulness
helping
helpless
helplessness
hemisphere
hemispherical
hence
henceforth
henchman
heptagon
heptagonal
her
Her Majesty's
    Stationery Office
    (HMSO)
herald
heraldic

heraldry
Herculean
herd
here
hereabouts
hereafter
hereby
hereditaments
hereditary
heredity
heresies
heresy
heretic
heretical
heretically
herewith
heritable property
heritage
hermaphrodite
hermetically
hers
herself
he's
hesitancy
hesitant
hesitate
hesitated
hesitating
hesitation
hexagon
hexagonal
hid
hidden
hide
hidebound
hiding
hierarchy
hieroglyphics
high
High Court
High Court of
    Justiciary

highbrow
higher
highest
high-jack
Highlands
highlight
highly
highness
highway
Highway Code
hijack
hijacked
hijacker
hijacking
hill
hilly
him
himself
hinc inde
hinder
hindered
hindering
hindrance
hindsight
hinge
hinged
hinging
hint
hip
hire
hire purchase
hired
hiring
his
historian
historic
historical
historically
histories
history
hit
hitch

hitches
hither
hitherto
hitting
hoard
hoarding
hoax
hoaxes
hoist
hold
holder
holder for value
holder in due course
holding
holding company
hold-up
hole
hollow
holocaust
holograph
holograph writ
holster
holt
holy
homage
home
Home Secretary
homed
homeless
homelessness
homeworker
homicidal
homicide
homing
homogenization
homogenize
homogenized
homogenizing
homologate
homologation
homonym
homosexual

hone
honed
honest
honesty
honeymoon
honing
honorarium
honorary
honorary sheriff
honour
honourable
honourably
honoured
honouring
hoodwink
hoof
hoofs
hook
hooked
hooligan
hooliganism
hoot
hooted
hooter
hooting
hooves
hope
hoped
hopeful
hopefully
hopefulness
hopeless
hopelessness
hoping
horde
horizon
horizontal
horning
horoscope
horrendous
horrible
horribly

horrified
horrify
horrifying
horror
horsepower
horticultural
horticulture
horticulturist
hose
hospitable
hospitably
hospital
hospitality
host
hostage
hostel
hostelries
hostelry
hostess
hostesses
hostile
hostile witness
hostilely
hostilities
hostility
hot
hotchpot
hotel
hot-headed
hotter
hottest
hound
hour
hourly
house
house bote
House of Commons
House of Lords
housebreaking
house-buyer
housed
household

householder
housekeeper
housekeeping
housewife
housing
housing association
housing benefit
hove to
hovel
hover
hovercraft
hovered
hovering
how
however
hub
hue and cry
huge
hugely
hugeness
hull
human
humane
humanely
humanism
humanist
humanitarian
humanity
humble
humbly
humiliate
humiliated
humiliating
humiliation
humility
humorist
humorous
humour
humus
hunch
hunches
hundred

hundredth
hundredweight
hung
hung jury
Hungarian
Hungary
hunt
hunter
hurried
hurry
hurrying
hurt
hurtful
hurtfully
husband
husbandry
hustings
hustle
hustled
hustling
hut
hybrid
hydrant
hydraulic
hydro
hydroelectric
hydrogen
hydrophobia
hygiene
hygienic
hygienically
hyperactive
hyperbole
hyperinflation
hyphen
hypnosis
hypnotic
hypnotically
hypnotism
hypnotist
hypnotize
hypnotized

hypnotizing
hypochondria
hypochondriac
hypocrisy
hypocrite
hypocritical
hypocritically
hypodermic
hypotenuse
hypothec
hypothecation
hypotheses
hypothesis
hypothetical
hypothetically
hysteria
hysterical
hysterically

Ii

I owe you (IOU)
ibidem (Ibid)
ice
iced
icy
I'd
id certum est quod
    certum reddi potest
id est (ie)
idea
ideal
idealism
idealist
idealize
idealized
idealizing

ideally
identical
identically
identification
identified
identify
identifying
identikit (picture)
identities
identity
ideological
ideologically
ideology
idiom
idiomatic
idiomatically
idiosyncrasies
idiosyncrasy
idiosyncratic
idiosyncratically
idle
idled
idleness
idling
idly
idol
idolize
idolized
idolizing
idyll
idyllic
idyllically
if
ignite
ignited
igniting
ignition
ignominious
ignominy
ignoramus
ignoramuses
ignorance

ignorant
ignorantia juris
    neminem excusat
ignore
ignored
ignoring
I'll
ill
illegal
illegally
illegibility
illegible
illegibly
illegitimacy
illegitimate
illegitimately
illicit
illiquid
illiteracy
illiterate
illness
illnesses
illogical
illogically
illuminate
illuminated
illuminating
illumination
illusion
illusory
illusory trust
illustrate
illustrated
illustrating
illustration
illustrative
illustrator
illustrious
I'm
image
imagery
imaginary

imagination
imaginative
imaginatively
imagine
imagined
imagining
imbecile
imbibe
imbibed
imbibing
imbue
imbued
imbuing
imitate
imitated
imitating
imitation
immaculate
immaculately
immaterial
immature
immediacy
immediate
immediately
immemorial
immense
immensely
immensity
immerse
immersed
immersing
immersion
immigrant
immigration
imminent
immobile
immobility
immobilize
immobilized
immobilizing
immoderate
immoral

immorality
immortal
immortality
immortalize
immortalized
immortalizing
immovable
immovably
immune
immunity
immunize
immunized
immunizing
impact
impair
impaired
impairing
impairment
impale
impaled
impaling
impart
impartial
impartiality
impartially
impassable
impasse
impassioned
impassive
impassively
impatience
impatient
impeach
impeachable waste
impeachment
impeccable
impeccably
impecunious
impede
impeded
impediment
impeding

impel
impelled
impelling
impending
imperative
imperatively
imperceptible
imperceptibly
imperfect
imperfect right
imperfection
imperial
imperialism
imperil
imperilled
imperilling
imperious
imperitia culpae
   adnumeratur
impermeable
impersonal
impersonally
impersonate
impersonated
impersonating
impersonation
impersonator
impertinence
impertinent
imperturbable
impervious
impetrate
impetuosity
impetuous
impetus
impiety
impignoration
impinge
impinged
impinging
impious
implead

implement
implicate
implicated
implicating
implication
implicit
implied
implied condition
implied contract
implied covenant
implied tenancy
implied term
imply
implying
impolite
impolitely
import
importance
important
importation
importer
importunate
importune
importuned
importuning
importunity
impose
imposed
imposing
imposition
impossibility
impossible
impossibly
impostor
impotence
impotent
impound
impoverish
impracticability
impracticable
impracticably
impractical

impracticality
impractically
impregnable
impregnate
impresario
impress
impressed
impression
impressionable
impressive
impressively
imprest
imprint
imprison
imprisoned
imprisoning
imprisonment
improbability
improbable
improbably
improbation
improbative
improper
improprieties
impropriety
improve
improved
improvement
improvidence
improvident
improving
improvisation
improvise
improvised
improvising
impudence
impudent
impulse
impulsive
impulsively
impulsiveness
impunity

impure
impurities
impurity
imputation
impute
imputed
imputing
in
in aequali jure melior
  est conditio
  possidentis
in alieno solo
in bonis
in camera
in causa
in esse
in extenso
in extremis
in flagrante delicto
in foro
in gremio
in gross
in hoc statu
in invitum
in lieu
in limine
in litem
in loco parentis
in medio
in meditatione fugae
in nomine
in pais
in pari causa
  possessor potior
  haberi debet
in pari delicto potior
  est conditio
  possidentis
in pari materia
in perpetum
in personam
in posse

in praesentia dominorum (IPD)
in re
in re mercatoria
in rem
in rem suam
in rem versum
in retentis
in situ
in solidum
in statu quo
in terrorem
in transitu
in verbis non verba sed res et ratio quaerenda est
inability
inaccessible
inaccessibly
inaccurate
inaccurately
inaction
inactive
inactivity
inadequacies
inadequacy
inadequate
inadequately
inadmissible
inadmissible evidence
inadvertence
inadvertent
inadvertent negligence
inalienability
inalienable
inane
inanely
inanimate
inanities
inanity
inapplicable

inappropriate
inappropriately
inapt
inarticulate
inasmuch as
inattention
inattentive
inattentively
inaudible
inaudibly
inaugural
inaugurate
inaugurated
inaugurating
inauguration
inauspicious
incalculable
incapable
incapacitate
incapacitated
incapacitating
incapacity
incapax
incarcerate
incarcerated
incarcerating
incendiarism
incendiary
incense
incensed
incensing
incentive
inception
incessant
incest
inch
inches
inchoate
incidence
incident
incidental
incidentally

incinerator
incipient
incision
incisive
incisively
incisiveness
incite
incited
incitement
incitement to disaffection
inciting
incivilities
incivility
inclemency
inclement
inclination
incline
inclined
inclining
inclosure
include
included
including
inclusio unius est exclusio alterius
inclusion
inclusive
inclusively
incognito
incoherence
incoherent
income
income tax
incoming
incommode
incommoded
incommoding
incommunicado
incomparable
incomparably
incompatibility

incompatible
incompetence
incompetent
incomprehensible
incomprehensibly
incomprehension
inconceivable
inconceivably
inconclusive
inconclusively
incongruity
incongruous
incongruously
inconsequential
inconsequentially
inconsiderable
inconsiderate
inconsiderately
inconsistent
inconspicuous
inconstancy
inconstant
incontrovertible
incontrovertibly
inconvenience
inconvenient
incorporate
incorporated
incorporating
incorporation
incorporeal
incorporeal
  hereditaments
incorporeal moveable
  property
incorrect
incorrigible
incorrigibly
incorruptible
increase
increased
increasing

increasingly
incredibility
incredible
incredibly
incredulity
incredulous
increment
incriminate
incriminated
incriminating
inculcate
inculcated
inculcating
incumbent
incumbrance
incur
incurable
incurably
incurred
incurring
incursion
indebted
indebtedness
indecency
indecent
indecision
indecisive
indecisively
indeed
indefatigable
indefatigably
indefeasible
indefensibly
indefinable
indefinably
indefinite
indefinitely
indelible
indelibly
indemnification
indemnify
indemnifying

indemnity
indent
indentation
indenture
independence
independent
indescribable
indescribably
indestructible
indeterminate
indeterminately
index
indexation
indexes
Indian
indicate
indicated
indicating
indication
indicative
indicator
indices
indict
indictable
indictment
indifference
indifferent
indigence
indigenous
indigent
indignant
indignation
indignities
indignity
indirect
indirect evidence
indiscreet
indiscretion
indiscriminate
indiscriminately
indispensable
indispensably

indisputable
indisputably
indistinct
indistinguishable
indistinguishably
individual
individualism
individualist
individuality
individually
indivisible
indivisible contract
indoctrinate
indoctrinated
indoctrinating
indorsement
indubitable
indubitably
induce
induced
inducement
induciae
inducing
induct
induction
inductive
indulge
indulged
indulgence
indulging
industrial
industrial espionage
industrial tribunal
industrialist
industrious
industry
inebriated
inebriation
ineffective
ineffectively
ineffectiveness
ineffectual

ineffectually
inefficiency
inefficient
ineligibility
ineligible
inept
ineptitude
inequalities
inequality
inert
inertia
inescapable
inescapably
inestimable
inestimably
inevitability
inevitable
inevitably
inexcusable
inexcusably
inexhaustible
inexorable
inexorably
inexpensive
inexpensively
inexperience
inexperienced
inexplicable
inexplicably
inexpressible
inexpressibly
inextricable
inextricably
infallibility
infallible
infamous
infamy
infancy
infant
infanticide
infatuated
infatuation

infect
infection
infectious
infeftment
infer
inference
inferential
inferior
inferior courts
inferiority
inferred
inferring
infertile
infertility
infidelity
infiltrate
infiltrated
infiltrating
infiltration
infinite
infinitely
infinitesimal
infinitesimally
infinitive
infirm
infirmaries
infirmary
infirmities
infirmity
inflammable
inflammatory
inflate
inflated
inflating
inflation
inflationary
inflexible
inflict
infliction
influence
influenced
influencing

influential
influentially
inform
informal
informality
informally
informant
information
informative
informatively
informed
informed consent
informer
infringe
infringed
infringement
infringing
ingather
ingross
inhabit
inhabitant
inhabited
inhabiting
inherent
inherent vice
inherit
inheritance
inheritance tax (IHT)
inherited
inheriting
inhibit
inhibited
inhibiting
inhibition
inhospitable
inhospitably
inhuman
inhumane
iniquities
iniquitous
iniquity
initial

initial writ
initialled
initialling
initially
initiate
initiated
initiating
initiation
initiative
inject
injection
injudicious
injunction
injure
injured
injuria
injuria non excusat
    injuriam
injuria sine damno
injuries
injuring
injurious affection
injurious falsehood
injury
injustice
ink
inkling
inland bill
Inland Revenue
inmate
inmost
inn
innate
inner
Inner House
Inner Temple
innocence
innocent
innocent
    misrepresentation
innocuous
innominate

innominate contract
innovation
Inns of Court
innuendo
innuendoes
innumerable
innumeracy
innumerate
inoculate
inoculated
inoculating
inoculation
inoffensive
inoffensively
inopportune
inopportunely
inordinate
inordinately
input
inquest
inquire
inquired
inquirer
inquiries
inquiring
inquiry
inquisition
inquisitive
inquisitively
inquisitor
inquisitorial
inroads
insane
insanely
insanitary
insanity
inscribe
inscribed
inscribing
inscription
insecticide
insecure

insecurely
insecurity
insensible
insensitive
insensitively
inseparable
inseparably
insert
insertion
inset
inshore
inside
insider dealing
insidious
insight
insignia
insignificance
insignificant
insincere
insincerely
insincerity
insinuate
insinuated
insinuating
insinuation
insist
insistence
insistent
insolence
insolent
insoluble
insolvency
insolvent
inspect
inspection
inspector
instability
instal
install
installation
installed
installing

instalment
instance
instant
instantaneous
instead
instigate
instigated
instigating
instigation
instil
instilled
instilling
institute
instituted
instituting
institution
institutional
instruct
instruction
instructive
instructively
instructor
instrument
instrumental
insubordinate
insubordination
insufficiency
insufficient
insult
insuperable
insuperably
insurable
insurance
insure
insured
insurer
insuring
insurmountable
insurmountably
intact
intake
intangible

intangible property
intangibly
integral
integrate
integrated
integrating
integration
integrity
intellect
intellectual
intellectual property
intellectually
intelligence
intelligent
intelligible
intelligibly
intend
intending
intense
intensely
intensified
intensify
intensifying
intensity
intensive
intensively
intent
intention
intentionally
inter
inter alia
inter alios
inter partes
inter se
inter vivos
interact
interaction
intercede
interceded
interceding
intercept
intercession

interchange
interchangeable
interchanged
interchanging
intercourse
interdict
interest
interest reipublicae ut
   sit finis litium
interesting
interfere
interfered
interference
interfering
interim
interim dividend
interim interdict
interim interlocutor
interior
interject
interjection
interline
interlineation
interlocutor
interlocutory appeal
intermediaries
intermediary
intermediate
interment
intermittent
intermixture
intern
internal
internally
international
internationally
internee
internment
interpleader summons
interpret
interpretation
interpreted

interpreter
interpreting
interred
interregnum
interring
interrogate
interrogated
interrogating
interrogation
interrogative
interrogator
interrogatories
interrupt
interruption
intersection
intersperse
interspersed
interspersing
interstice
interval
intervene
intervened
intervener
intervening
intervening cause
intervention
interview
intestacy
intestate
intestinal
intestines
intimacy
intimate
intimated
intimately
intimating
intimation
intimidate
intimidated
intimidating
intimidation
into

intolerable
intolerably
intolerance
intolerant
intoxicant
intoxicate
intoxicated
intoxicating
intoxication
intra vires
intractable
intransigence
intransigent
intransitive
intricacies
intricacy
intricate
intricately
intrigue
intrigued
intriguing
intrinsic
intrinsic evidence
intrinsically
introduce
introduced
introducing
introduction
introductory
intromission
intromit
intromitter
intrude
intruded
intruder
intruding
intrusion
intrusive
intrusively
inure
inured
inuring

invalid
invalidate
invalidated
invalidating
invalidity
invaluable
invaluably
invariable
invariably
invasion
invecta et illata
invective
inveigle
inveigled
inveigling
invent
invention
inventive
inventor
inventories
inventory
inventory of process
inventory of
   deceased's estate
inverse
inversely
inversion
invert
invest
investigate
investigated
investigating
investigation
investigator
investiture
investment
investor
inveterate
invidious
inviolable
inviolate
invisibility

invisible
invisibly
invitee
invocation
invoice
invoke
invoked
invoking
involuntarily
involuntary
involve
involved
involvement
involving
inward
inwardly
inwards
ipse dixit
ipso facto
ipso jure
Iranian
Iraqui
irascibility
irascible
irascibly
irate
irately
ire
Irish
irk
irksome
ironic
ironical
ironically
ironies
irony
irradiate
irrational
irrationally
irrebuttable
   presumption
irregular

irregular marriage
irregularities
irregularity
irrelevance
irrelevancy
irrelevant
irrelevant evidence
irreparable
irreparably
irreplaceable
irresistible
irresolute
irresolutely
irrespective
irrespectively
irresponsible
irresponsibly
irretrievable
   breakdown
irreverence
irreverent
irrevocable
irrevocably
irritancy
irritant
is
ish
island company
isn't
isolate
isolated
isolating
isolation
Israeli
issue
issue estoppel
issue of shares at a
   discount
issued
issued capital
issuing
isthmus

isthmuses
it
Italian
italics
item
itemise
iter
itinerant
itineraries
itinerary
it'll
it's
its
itself
I've

Jj

jab
jabbed
jabbing
jacket
jack-knife
Jacuzzi®
jail
jailer
jamb
janitor
January
jar
jargon
jarred
jarring
jaundice
jaunt
jauntily
jaunty
jaw

jaywalker
jealous
jealousy
jeep
jeer
jeered
jeering
jeopardize
jeopardized
jeopardizing
jeopardy
jerk
jerkily
jerky
jet
jetsam
jetties
jettison
jettisoned
jettisoning
jetty
Jew
jewel
jeweller
jewellery
Jewish
jib
jibbed
jibbing
jibe
jibed
jibing
jilt
job
Job Centre
jobber
jobbing
jockey
jockeyed
jockeying
jocular
jocularity

jog
jogged
jogging
join
joinder
joined
joiner
joining
joint
joint adventure
joint and several
joint and several
    liability
joint and several
    obligation
joint heir
joint obligation
joint property
joint stock company
joint tenancy
joint torfeasors
jointly and severally
jointress
jointure
joist
joke
joked
joker
joking
jolt
jostle
jostled
jostling
jot
jotted
jotter
jotting
journal
journalism
journalist
journey
journeyed

Kk

journeying
jovial
jovially
jowl
joy
joy riding
joyful
joyfully
joyfulness
joyless
joyous
judge
judge advocate
Judge Advocate-
  General
judged
judgement
judging
judgment
judicatum solvi
judicial
judicial audits
judicial cognisance
Judicial Committee of
  the Privy Council
  (JCPC)
judicial discretion
judicial examination
judicial factor
judiciary
judicio sisti
judicious
judicis est jus dicere,
  non dare
jug
juggernaut
juggle
juggled
juggling
jugular
ju-jitsu
July

jumble
jumbled
jumbling
jump
jumpy
junction
juncture
June
jungle
junior
junior counsel
junk
junk bond
jura in personam
jura in re propria
jura in rem
jurat
juridical
juries
jurimetrics
juris et de jure
jurisdiction
jurisdictional
jurisdictionis
  fundandae causa
jurisprudence
juristic
juristic person
juror
jury
jury trial
jus
jus ad rem
jus civile
jus crediti
jus dicere
jus disponendi
jus gentium
jus in personam
jus in re
jus in re aliena
jus naturale

jus paseendi
jus quaesitum tertio
jus relictae
jus relicti
jus soli
jus tertii
just
just and equitable
justice
Justice (J)
Justice of the Peace
  (JP)
justifiable
justifiable homicide
justifiably
justification
justified
justify
justifying
jut
jute
jutted
jutting
juvenile
juxtapose
juxtaposed
juxtaposing
juxtaposition

Kk

kale
kaleidoscope
kaleidoscopic
kaleidoscopically
kangaroo court
kapok
karate

keel
keeled
keeling
keen
keenness
keep
keeper
keeping
keeping term
keeping the peace
keepsake
keg
kennel
kept
kerb
kerb-crawling
kernel
kerosene
key
keyboard
keyed-up
keyhole
keynote
khaki
kick
kick-off
kid
kidnap
kidnapped
kidnapper
kidnapping
kidney
kill
killer
killing
kilogram
kilogramme
kilometre
kilowatt
kilt
kin
kind

kindergarten
kindle
kindled
kindliness
kindling
kindly
kindly tenant
kindness
kindred
kinetic
kinetically
king
kingdom
King's Bench (KB)
King's Counsel (KC)
kinsman
kiosk
Kirk-Session
kiss
kisses
kit
kitchen
kitchenette
kleptomania
kleptomaniac
knack
knapsack
knave
knavish
knead
knee
kneed
kneeing
kneel
kneeling
knell
knelt
knew
knife
knifed
knifing
knight

knighted
knighthood
knives
knob
knock
knock for knock
knocker
knock-out agreement
knoll
knot
knotted
knotting
knotty
know
know-how
knowing
knowingly
knowledge
knowledgeable
knowledgeably
known
knuckle
knuckled
knuckling
Koran
kosher
kowtow
kowtowed
kowtowing
kudos
kung fu

Ll

la reyne le veult
la reyne s'avisera
lab
label

91

labelled
labelling
labes realis
laboratories
laboratory
laborious
labour
laboured
labourer
labouring
labyrinth
lace
laced
lacerate
lacerated
lacerating
laceration
laches
lacing
lack
lackadaisical
lackadaisically
lackey
laconic
laconically
lacquer
lacquered
lacquering
lactic
lacuna
lad
ladder
laddered
laddering
lade
laden
ladies
lading
ladle
ladled
ladling
lady

Lady Day
ladyship
lag
lagged
lagging
laid
lain
lair
laird
laissez faire
laity
lake
lame
lameness
lament
lamentable
lamentation
Lammas
lance
lance-corporal
lanced
lancing
land
land certificate
land register
land registration
Land Registry
land tax
land tenure
landladies
landlady
landlord
Lands Tribunal
landscape
lane
language
languid
languish
laniard
lank
lanky
lantern

lanyard
lap
lapel
lapidaries
lapidary
lapped
lapping
lapse
lapsed
lapsing
larceny
larder
large
largely
largeness
largesse
laryngitis
larynx
lascivious
laser
lash
lashes
lassitude
lasso
lassoes
lassos
last
lastly
latch
latches
latchkey
late
lately
latency
lateness
latent
latent ambiguity
latent damage
latent defect
lateral
laterally
latex

lath
lathe
lather
lathered
lathering
Latin
latitude
latter
latterly
lattice
laud
laudable
laudably
lauded
lauding
laugh
laughable
laughably
laughter
launch
launches
launder
laundered
launderette
laundering
laundries
laundry
lavatories
lavatory
lavish
law
law agent
law burrows
Law Commission
Law Lord
law merchant
Law Reform
    Committee
Law Reports
Law Society
lawburrow
lawful

lawfully
lawless
lawlessness
lawsuit
lawyer
lax
laxative
laxity
lay
lay days
lay magistrate
lay observer
layabout
layby
layer
laying
laying an information
laze
lazed
lazier
laziest
lazily
laziness
lazing
lazy
lead
lead evidence
leaden
leader
leading
leading case
leading question
leaflet
league
leak
leakage
lean
leaned
leaning
leanness
leant
leap

leaped
leaping
leapt
learn
learned
learner
learning
learnt
lease
leaseback
leased
leasehold
leash
leashes
leasing
least
leather
leave
leaving
lecherous
lechery
lectern
lecture
lectured
lecturer
lecturing
led
ledge
ledger
leer
leered
leering
leeway
left
leg
legacies
legacy
legal
legal aid
legal easement
legal estate
legal lease

legal leasehold estate
legal person
legal personality
legal rights
legalise
legalities
legality
legalize
legalized
legalizing
legally
legatee
legation
legerdemain
legibility
legible
legibly
legion
legionary
legislate
legislated
legislating
legislation
legislative
legislator
legislature
legitim
legitimacy
legitimate
legitimately
legitimation
leisure
leisured
leisurely
lend
lending
length
lengthen
lengthened
lengthening
lengthily
lengthways

lengthy
leniency
lenient
lenocinium
lens
lenses
Lent
lent
leonina societas
lesbian
lesbianism
lesion
less
lessee
lessen
lessened
lessening
lesser
lesson
lessor
lest
let
lethal
lethargic
lethargically
lethargy
letter
letter of credit
lettered
lettering
letters of inhibition
letting
leukaemia
levant and couchant
levari facias
level
levelled
levelling
lever
levied
levies
levity

levy
levying
lewd
lewdness
lex causae
lex domicilii
lex fori
lex loci actus
lex loci contractus
lex loci delicti
    commissi
lex loci situs
lex loci solutionis
lex talionis
lexicographer
lexicography
liabilities
liability
liable
liaise
liaised
liaising
liaison
liar
libel
libelled
libelling
libellous
liberal
liberality
liberally
liberate
liberated
liberating
liberation
liberties
libertine
liberty
librarian
libraries
library
lice

licence
licence by estoppel
license
licensed
licensed conveyancer
licensee
licensing
licentious
licentiousness
lick
lid
lie
lie in grant
lie in livery
lied
liege
lien
lieu
lieutenant
life
life annuity
life assurance
life estate
life interest
life policy
lifeguard
lifeless
life-like
liferent
liferenter
lift
lifting the corporate
  veil
lift-off
ligament
ligature
light
lighted
lighten
lightened
lightening
lighter

lighthouse
lighting
likable
like
likeable
liked
likelihood
likely
likeness
likewise
liking
limb
limber
limbered
limbering
limbo
limelight
limit
limitation
limitation of actions
limited
limited administration
limited company
limited executor
limited liability
limited partnership
limiting
limousine
limp
linchpin
Lincoln's Inn
line
lineage
lineal
lineal ancestor
lineal consanguinity
lineal descendant
lineal descent
lineally
lineament
linear
lined

liner
linesman
linger
lingered
lingerie
lingering
linguist
linguistic
linguistically
liniment
lining
link
linked transaction
linoleum
lintel
lionize
lionized
lionizing
lip
lipstick
liquefied
liquefy
liquefying
liqueur
liquid
liquidate
liquidated
liquidated damages
liquidated demand
liquidating
liquidation
liquidator
liquidity
liquor
lis
lis alibi pendens
lis mota
lis pendens
lisp
list
listed building
listed securities

listen
listened
listener
listening
listless
lit
litanies
litany
lite pendente
literacy
literal
literally
literary
literate
literature
lithe
lithograph
litigant
litigate
litigation
litigiosity
litigious
litiscontestation
litre
litter
littered
littering
little
liturgical
liturgies
liturgy
live
lived
livelier
liveliest
livelihood
lively
liven up
livened up
livening up
liver
liveries

livery
lives
livestock
livid
living
living-room
Lloyd's
load
loaf
loafed
loafing
loam
loan
loan capital
loath
loathe
loathed
loathing
lob
lobbed
lobbies
lobbing
lobby
lobe
loc cit loco citato
local
local authority
Local Government
    Ombudsman
local land charge
locale
locality
localize
localized
localizing
locate
located
locating
locatio conductio
locatio operarum
locatio operis faciendi
locatio rei

location
loch
lock
locker
locket
lockfast place
lockjaw
lock-out
loco citato
loco parentis
loco tutoris
locomotion
locomotive
locum
locum tenens
locus
locus in quo
locus poenitentiae
locus regit actum
locus sigilli
locus standi
lodestar
lodestone
lodge
lodged
lodger
lodging
loftily
loftiness
lofty
log
logbook
logged
loggerheads
logging
logic
logical
logically
logo
loiter
loitered
loitering

loll
lolled
lolling
London Gazette
lone
loneliness
lonely
long
long negative prescription
long tenancy
long title
longevity
longing
longitude
look
lookout
loom
loomed
looming
loop
looped
loophole
looping
loose
loosely
loosen
loosened
loosening
loot
looter
looting
lop
lopped
lopping
lop-sided
loquacious
lord
Lord Advocate
Lord Chancellor (LC)
Lord Chief Justice (LCJ)

Lord Clerk Register
Lord High Commissioner
Lord High Constable
Lord Justice Clerk
Lord Justice General
Lord Justice of Appeal (LJ)
Lord Lieutenant of the County
Lord Lyon King of Arms
Lord of Appeal in Ordinary
Lord Ordinary
Lord President
Lord Privy Seal
Lord Spiritual
Lord Temporal
lordly
lordship
lore
lorgnette
lorries
lorry
lose
loser
losing
loss
loss leaders
loss of amenity
losses
lost
lost capital
lost modern grant
lot
loth
lotion
lotteries
lottery
loud
loudness

loudspeaker
lounge
lounged
lounging
lour
louse
lout
lovable
love
loved
lovelier
loveliest
loveliness
lovely
lover
loving
low
lower
lowered
lowering
lowland
lowliness
lowly
lowness
loyal
loyalist
loyally
loyalty
lozenge
ls locus sigilli
lubricant
lubricate
lubricated
lubricating
lubrication
lucid
lucid interval
lucidity
luck
luckier
luckiest
luckily

lucky
lucrative
lucre
lucri causa
ludicrous
lug
luggage
lugged
lugging
lugubrious
lukewarm
lull
lulled
lulling
lumbago
lumbar
lumber
lumbered
lumbering
luminosity
luminous
lump
lump cum contract
lump sum award
lumpy
lunacy
lunar
lunatic
lung
lunge
lunged
lunging
lurch
lure
lured
lurid
luring
lurk
luscious
lush
lust
lustful

lustfully
lustily
lustre
lustrous
lusty
luxuriant
luxuriate
luxuriated
luxuriating
luxuries
luxurious
luxury
lying
lymph gland
lynch

Mm

macabre
mace
macer
Mach number
machination
machine
machinery
machinery and plant
machinist
macroeconomics
mad
madam
madden
maddened
maddening
madder
maddest
made
Madeira
madman

madmen
madness
Madonna
maelstrom
maestro
magazine
magic
magical
magically
magician
magisterial
magistrate
Magna Carta
magnanimity
magnanimous
magnate
magnesium
magnet
magnetic
magnetically
magnetism
magnetization
magnetize
magnetized
magnetizing
magnification
magnificence
magnificent
magnified
magnify
magnifying
magnitude
Maharajah
mahogany
maid
mail
mailed
mailing
maills and duties
maim
maimed
maiming

Mm

main
main residence
mainframe
mainland
mainly
mainsail
mainstay
maintain
maintained
maintaining
maintenance
majestic
majestically
majesties
majesty
major
majorities
majority
majority verdict
make
maker
makeshift
make-up
making
mala fide
mala fides
mala in se
mala praxis
mala prohibita
maladies
maladjusted
maladministration
malady
malaise
malapropism
malaria
male
male appretiata
male issue
malevolence
malevolent
malfeasance

malformation
malformed
malice
malice aforethought
malice prepense
malicious
malicious arrest
malicious mischief
malign
malignant
maligned
maligning
malinger
malingered
malingerer
malingering
malitia supplet
  aetatem
malleable
mallet
malnutrition
malodorous
malpractice
maltreat
maltreatment
malversation
man
man of straw
manacle
manage
manageable
managed
management
manager
manageress
managing
managing director
mandamus
mandate
mandatory
mandible
manful

manfully
mangle
mangled
mangling
manhandle
manhandled
manhandling
manhood
mania
maniac
maniacal
manic
manifest
manifestation
manifesto
manifestoes
manifestos
manifold
manipulate
manipulated
manipulating
manipulation
mankind
manned
manner
mannerism
mannerly
manning
mannish
manoeuvre
manor
manorial
manpower
manse
mansion
manslaughter
mansuetae naturae
manual
manual labour
manually
manufacture
manufactured

manufacturer
manufacturing
manuscript
many
map
mapped
mapping
mar
maraud
marauder
marauding
marble
March
march
marches
marchioness
marchionesses
Mareva injunction
margin
marginal
marginally
marijuana
marina
marine
marine adventure
marine waters
mariner
marital
maritime
maritime lien
maritime perils
mark
mark-down
marked
marker
market
market overt
market price
market value
marketed
marketing
mark-up

maroon
marooned
marooning
marquee
marquess
marquesses
marquis
marquises
marred
marriage
marriage articles
marriage brokage
marriage brokage
   contract
marriage
   consideration
marriage-contract
marriage of
   convenience
marriage settlement
marriageable
marrièd
marring
marry
marrying
marsh
marshal
marshall
marshalled
marshalling
marshes
marshy
martial
martial law
martinet
Martinmas
martyr
martyrdom
martyred
martyring
marvel
marvelled

marvelling
marvellous
mascot
masculine
masculinity
mash
mask
masochism
masochist
masochistic
masochistically
mason
masonic
masonry
masquerade
masqueraded
masquerader
masquerading
mass
massacre
massacred
massacring
massage
massaged
massaging
masses
masseur
masseuse
massive
mast
master
Master of the Bench
Master of the Crown
   Office
Master of the Rolls
   (MR)
Master of the
   Supreme Court
masterful
masterfully
masterliness
masterly

masterpiece
mastery
masticate
masticated
masticating
mastication
mastiff
masturbate
masturbated
masturbating
mat
match
matches
matchless
mate
mated
material
material fact
materialism
materialistic
materialistically
materialization
materialize
materialized
materializing
materially
maternal
maternally
maternity
maternity leave
maternity pay
mathematical
mathematically
mathematician
mathematics
mating
matrices
matricide
matriculate
matriculated
matriculating
matriculation

matrimonial
matrimonial cause
matrimonial home
matrimony
matrix
matron
matronly
matt
matte
matted
matter
mattered
mattering
matter-of-fact
matting
mattress
mattresses
mature
matured
maturing
maturity
maudlin
maul
mauled
mauling
mausoleum
mawkish
maxim
maxima
maximum
May
may
maybe
mayday
mayhem
mayor
mayoress
maze
McKenzie man
me
meadow
meagre

meagrely
meal
mean
meander
meandered
meandering
meaning
meaningful
meaningfully
meaningless
meanness
meant
meanwhile
measure
measured
measurement
measuring
meat
meaty
Mecca
mechanic
mechanical
mechanically
mechanics
mechanism
mechanization
mechanize
mechanized
mechanizing
medal
medallion
medallist
meddle
meddled
meddler
meddling
media
mediaeval
mediate
mediated
mediating
mediation

mediator
medical
medically
medicated
medication
medicinal
medicine
medieval
mediocre
mediocrity
meditate
meditated
meditating
meditation
Mediterranean
medium
medium concludendi
meek
meet
meeting
megalomania
megaphone
melancholic
melancholy
melior est conditio
   possidentis et rei
   quam actoris
meliorations
mellifluous
mellow
melodic
melodies
melodious
melodrama
melodramatic
melodramatically
melody
melt
member
Member of Parliament
   (MP)
membership

membrane
memento
memo
memoir
memorable
memorably
memoranda
memorandum
memorandum of
   association
memorial
memories
memorize
memorized
memorizing
memory
men
menace
menaced
menaces
menacing
ménage
menagerie
mend
mendacious
mendacity
mendicant
menial
meningitis
mens rea
menstrual
menstruate
menstruated
menstruating
menstruation
mental
mental disorder
mental distress
Mental Health
   Commission
mental illness
mental patient

mentalities
mentality
mentally
menthol
mention
mentioned
mentioning
mentor
mercantile
mercenaries
mercenary
merchandise
merchant
merchantable quality
merciful
mercifully
merciless
mercurial
mercury
mercy
mercy killing
mere
merely
merge
merged
merger
merging
meridian
merit
merited
meriting
meritorious
merits
mesh
meshes
mesmerism
mesmerize
mesmerized
mesmerizing
mesne
mesne profits
mess

message
messenger
messenger-at-arms
messes
Messrs
messuage
met
metal
metallic
metallurgical
metallurgy
metamorphoses
metamorphosis
metaphor
metaphorical
metaphorically
mete out
meted out
meteor
meteoric
meteorite
meteorological
meteorologically
meteorologist
meteorology
meter
metes and bounds
method
methodical
methodically
methylated spirits
meticulous
meting out
metre
metric
metrical
metricate
metricated
metricating
metrication
metropolis
metropolises

metropolitan
mettle
mews
mezzanine
mice
Michaelmas Day
microbe
microchip
microcomputer
microcosm
microeconomics
microfiche
microfilm
microphone
microprocessor
microscope
microscopic
microsurgery
microwave
mid-couples
midday
middle
Middle Temple
middle-aged
middle-class
middleman
middling
midescription
midget
mid-impediment
midnight
midriff
midst
Midsummer Day
midway
midwife
midwifery
midwives
mien
might
mightier
mightiest

mightily
mightiness
mighty
migraine
migrant
migrate
migrated
migrating
migratory
milage
mild
mildew
mile
mileage
milestone
milieu
militant
military
military testament
militate
militated
militating
militia
milk
milky
mill
millennia
millennium
miller
millet
milligramme
millilitre
millimetre
million
millionaire
mime
mimed
mimic
mimicked
mimicking
mimicry
miming

Mm

mince
minced
mincing
mind
mindful
mindless
mine
miner
mineral
mineralogical
mineralogically
mineralogist
mineralogy
mingle
mingled
mingling
miniature
minicomputer
minima
minimal
minimize
minimized
minimizing
minimum
minimum subscription
minion
minister
ministered
ministerial
ministerially
ministerial
   responsibility
ministering
ministries
ministry
mink
minor
minor interests
minorities
minority
minority and lesion
minority shareholder

minus
minute
minute-book
miracle
miraculous
mirage
mire
mirror
mirrored
mirroring
mirth
misadventure
misanthropist
misanthropy
misappropriate
misappropriation
misbehave
misbehaved
misbehaving
misbehaviour
miscarriage
miscarried
miscarry
miscarrying
miscellaneous
miscellanies
miscellany
mischance
mischief
mischievous
misconception
misconduct
miscreant
misdeed
misdemeanour
misdirection
miser
miserable
miserably
miseries
miserly
misery

misfeasance
misfire
misfired
misfiring
misfit
misfortune
misgiving
misguided
mishap
misjoinder of parties
mislaid
mislay
mislaying
mislead
misleading
misled
misnomer
misogynist
mispleading
misprint
misprision of treason
misrepresent
misrepresentation
miss
missed
misses
misshapen
missile
missing
mission
missionaries
missionary
missive
missive of sale
misspell
misspelled
misspelling
misspelt
misspent
mistake
mistake of law
mistaken

mistaking
mister
mistook
mistress
mistresses
mistrial
mistrust
misunderstand
misunderstanding
misunderstood
misuse
mite
mitigate
mitigated
mitigating
mitigation
mitre
mittimus
mix
mixed action
mixed fund
mixed property
mixer
mixes
mixture
M'Naghten Rules
mnemonic
moan
moaned
moaning
moat
mob
mobbed
mobbing
mobbing and rioting
mobile
mobility
mobilization
mobilize
mobilized
mobilizing
mock

mock auction
mockery
mocking
mode
model
modelled
modelling
moderate
moderately
moderation
moderator
modern
modernity
modernization
modernize
modernized
modernizing
modest
modesty
modicum
modification
modified
modify
modifying
modulate
modulated
modulating
modulation
module
modus operandi
modus vivendi
Mohammedan
moiety
moist
moisten
moistened
moistening
moisture
moisturize
moisturized
moisturizing
molecular

molecule
molest
molestation
mollified
mollify
mollifying
mollycoddle
mollycoddled
mollycoddling
molten
moment
momentarily
momentary
momentous
momentum
monarch
monarchies
monarchy
monasteries
monastery
monastic
monasticism
Monday
monetarism
monetary
money
moneyed
moneylender
money-lending
mongrel
monied
monitor
monitored
monitoring
monogamous
monogamy
monogram
monologue
monopolies
Monopolies and
   Mergers
   Commission (MMC)

Mm

monopolize
monopolized
monopolizing
monopoly
monosyllabic
monosyllable
monotone
monotonous
monotony
monster
monstrosities
monstrosity
monstrous
month
monthlies
monthly
monument
monumental
mood
moody
moor
moored
mooring
moot
moot point
mop
mope
moped
moping
mopped
mopping
mora
moral
morale
morality
moralize
moralized
moralizing
morally
morass
morasses
moratorium

morbid
morbidity
more
moreover
morgue
moribund
morning
moron
moronic
morose
morosely
morphia
morse
morsel
mortal
mortality
mortally
mortar
mortgage
mortgaged
mortgagee
mortgaging
mortgagor
mortice
mortification
mortified
mortify
mortifying
mortis causa
mortuaries
mortuary
Moslem
mosque
most
mostly
mote
mother
mothered
motherhood
mothering
mother-in-law
motherliness

motherly
motion
motion roll
motionless
motivate
motivated
motivating
motive
motley
motor
motor car
motor vehicle
motor-bike
motorcycle
motorist
motorize
motorized
motorizing
motorway
mottled
motto
mottoes
mould
moulder
mouldering
mouldy
mound
mount
mountain
mountaineer
mountainous
mourn
mourner
mournful
mournfully
mourning
moustache
mousy
mouth
mouthed
mouthful
mouthing

movable
movables
move
moveable
moveable estate
moveable property
moveables
moved
movement
moving
mow
mowed
mower
mowing
Mr
Mrs
Ms
much
muck
mucous
mucus
muddle
muddled
muddling
muddy
mudguard
muffle
muffled
muffler
muffling
mug
mugged
mugger
mugging
muirburn
mulatto
mull
multi-coloured
multifarious
multimillionaire
multinational
multiple

multiple admissibility
multiple damages
multiplepoinding
multiplex
multiplication
multiplicity
multiplicity of issues
multiplied
multiply
multiplying
multitude
multitudinous
multum in parvo
multures
multures
mumble
mumbled
mumbling
mundane
municipal
municipalities
municipality
munificence
munificent
muniments
munitions
munus publicum
mural
murder
murdered
murderer
murdering
murderous
murky
murmur
murmured
murmuring
muscle
muscular
muse
mused
museum

mushroom
mushroomed
mushrooming
music
musical
musically
musician
musing
Muslim
must
muster
mustered
mustering
musty
mutatis mutandis
mute
muted
mutilate
mutilated
mutilating
mutilation
mutineer
mutinied
mutinies
mutinous
mutiny
mutinying
mutter
muttered
muttering
mutual
mutual dealings
mutual desertion
mutual gable
mutual wills
mutually
mutuum
muzzle
muzzled
muzzling
muzzy
my

myopia
myopic
myopically
myriad
myself
mysteries
mysterious
mystery
mystic
mystically
mystified
mystify
mystifying
mystique
myth
mythical
mythically
mythological
mythology
myxomatosis

nag
nagged
nagging
nail
nailed
nailing
naïve
naïveté
naked
naked contract
naked trust
name
named
namely
naming

nape
narcotic
narrate
narrated
narrating
narration
narrative
narrator
narrow
nasal
nastily
nastiness
nasty
natal
natarise
nation
national
National Health
    Service (NHS)
national insurance
National Insurance
    Tribunals
nationalism
nationalities
nationality
nationalization
nationalize
nationalized
nationalizing
nationally
native
natural
natural allegiance
natural child
natural justice
natural law
natural person
natural rights
natural use
naturalisation
naturalist
naturalize

naturalized
naturalizing
naturally
nature
naughtily
naughtiness
naughty
nausea
nauseate
nauseated
nauseating
nauseous
nautical
naval
navies
navigable
navigate
navigated
navigating
navigation
navigator
navy
ne exeat regno
near
nearly
nearness
neat
nebulous
nec vi, nec clam, nec
    precario
necessaries
necessarily
necessary
necessitate
necessitated
necessitating
necessities
necessity
neck
née
need
needful

needless
needy
nefarious
negate
negated
negating
negative
negative clearance
negative pregnant
negative prescription
negative servitude
neglect
neglectful
negligence
negligent
negligent
  misrepresentation
negligent
  misstatement
negligible
negligibly
negotiable
negotiable instrument
negotiate
negotiated
negotiating
negotiation
negotiator
negotiorum gestio
Negress
Negro
Negroes
negroid
neighbour
neighbourhood
neighbouring
neighbourliness
neighbourly
neither
nem con
nemesis
nemine contradicente

nemo dat quod non
  habet
nemo debet bis puniri
  pro uno delicto
nemo debet bis vexari
nemo debet esse
  judex in propria
  causa
nemo est heres
  viventis
nemo tenetur seipsum
  accusare
nephew
nerve
nervous
nervousness
nervy
net
net annual value
net assets
net estate
nether
nethermost
nett
netted
netting
network
neuralgia
neuroses
neurosis
neurotic
neuter
neutered
neutering
neutral
neutrality
neutralize
neutralized
neutralizing
neutrally
neutron
never

nevertheless
new
new trial
newly
newness
news
newspaper
next
next friend
next-of-kin
nib
nice
nicely
niceties
nicety
niche
nickel
nickname
nicotine
niece
niggardly
niggling
night
nightly
nightmare
nil
nimble
nimbly
nimious and
  oppressive
nine
nineteen
nineteenth
ninetieth
ninety
ninth
nip
nipped
nipping
nipple
nisi
nisi prius (NP)

nitrate
nitric
nitrogen
no
no case to answer
nobile officium
nobility
noble
nobly
nobody
no-claims bonus
nocturnal
nocturnally
nod
nodded
nodding
node
nodule
noes
noise
noisily
noisy
nolens volens
nolle prosequi
nolo contendere
nom de plume
nomad
nomadic
nomenclature
nominal
nominal capital
nominal damages
nominal partner
nominal raiser
nominally
nominate
nominated
nominating
nomination
nominee
noms de plume
non assumpsit

non compos mentis
non constat
non est factum
non est inventus
non haec in foedera
   veni
non obstante
non obstante
   veredicto
non placet
non prosequitur
non sequitur
non valens agere
nonage
nonagenarian
nonchalance
nonchalant
non-committal
nonconformist
nondescript
non-direction
non-disclosure
none
nonentities
nonentity
nonfeasance
non-joinder
non-judicial audits
nonplussed
nonsense
nonsensical
nonsensically
non-suit
non-user
non-voting
no-one
noose
nor
norm
normal
normally
north

northerly
northern
Norwegian
noscitur a sociis
nose
nostalgia
nostalgic
nostalgically
nostril
not
not guilty
not negotiable
not proven
notabilities
notability
notable
notably
notarial execution
notarial instrument
notaries public
notary
notary public (NP)
notation
notch
notches
note
noted
noteworthy
nothing
notice
notice of title
notice to quit
noticeable
noticeably
noticed
noticing
notifiable
notification
notified
notify
notifying
noting

noting a bill
notion
notoriety
notorious
notorious facts
notour bankrupt
notour bankruptcy
notwithstanding
nought
noun
nourish
nourishment
nova causa
  interveniens
nova debita
novation
novel
novelist
novelties
novelty
November
novice
novodamus
novus actus
  interveniens
now
nowadays
nowhere
noxious
nozzle
nuance
nuclear
nuclear installation
nuclei
nude
nudist
nudity
nudum pactum
nuisance
nul tiel
null
null and void

nulla bona
nulla poena sine lege
nullified
nullify
nullifying
nullity
nullum crimen sine
  lege
nullum tempus
  occurrit regi
numb
number
numbered
numbering
numbskull
numeracy
numeral
numerate
numerical
numerically
numerous
numskull
nun
nunc pro tunc
nuncupative
nuncupative will
nunneries
nunnery
nunquam indebitatus
nuptial
nurse
nursed
nurseries
nursery
nursing
nurture
nurtured
nurturing
nutrient
nutriment
nutrition
nutritious
nylon

Oo

oaf
oath
oath of allegiance
oath of credulity
ob contingentiam
ob non solutum
  canonem
obduracy
obdurate
obdurately
obedience
obedient
obediential
obeisance
obese
obesity
obey
obeyed
obeying
obiter
obiter dictum or dicta
obituaries
obituary
object
objection
objectionable
objectionably
objective
objectively
objects of a power
objet d'art
objets d'art
obligant
obligation
obligationes literi
obligatorily
obligatory
oblige

obliged
obligee
obliging
obligor
oblique
obliterate
obliterated
obliterating
obliteration
oblivion
oblivious
oblong
obnoxious
obscene
obscenely
obscenities
obscenity
obscure
obscurely
obscurity
obsequious
observance
observant
observation
observatories
observatory
observe
observed
observer
observing
obsess
obsession
obsessive
obsessively
obsolescence
obsolescent
obsolete
obstacle
obstetrical
obstetrician
obstetrics
obstinacy

obstinate
obstinately
obstreperous
obstruct
obstruction
obtain
obtainable
obtained
obtaining
obtemper
obtrusive
obtrusively
obtuse
obtusely
obviate
obviated
obviating
obvious
obviously
occasion
occasional
occasionally
occult
occupancy
occupant
occupatio
occupation
occupation road
occupational pension
occupied
occupier
occupy
occupying
occupying tenant
occur
occurred
occurrence
occurring
ocean
o'clock
octagonal
octagonally

October
octogenarian
ocular
oculist
odd
oddities
oddity
oddment
odious
odium
odour
odourless
of
off
off-chance
offence
offend
offender
offensive
offensive trade
offensive weapon
offensively
offer
offer for sale
offered
offering
offhand
office
office of profit
officer
officers of state
official
Official Petitioner
official receiver
official referee
official search
official secrets
Official Solicitor
officially
officiate
officiated
officiating

officious
offing
off-licence
off-market deal
offset
offsetting
offshoot
offspring
often
ogle
ogled
ogling
oil
oiled
oilfield
oiling
oilrig
oily
ointment
old
Old Bailey
old-fashioned
oligopoly
ombudsman
omega
omen
ominous
omissa
omission
omit
omitted
omitting
omne quod solo
 inaedificatur solo
 cedit
omnia praesumuntur
 contra spoliatorem
omnia praesumuntur
 rite et solemniter
 esse acta
omnibus
omnibuses

omnipotent
omniscient
on
on bail
once
oncoming
one
oneris ferendi
onerous
oneself
ongoing
onlooker
only
onslaught
onus
onus probandi
onwards
ooze
oozed
oozing
opacity
opaque
ope et concilio
open
open contract
open court
open record
open verdict
opened
opener
opening
opening speech
openly
opera
operate
operated
operating
operation
operative
operative mistake
operator
ophthalmic

ophthalmologist
opiate
opinion
opinionated
opium
opponent
opportune
opportunism
opportunist
opportunities
opportunity
oppose
opposed
opposing
opposite
opposition
oppress
oppression
oppressive
opprobrious
opprobrium
opt
optical
optician
optimism
optimist
optimistic
optimistically
optimum
option
optional
optionally
opulence
opulent
opus
or
oracle
oral
oral agreement
oral evidence
orality
orally

oration
orator
oratories
oratory
orb
orbit
orbited
orbiting
orchard
orchestra
ordain
ordeal
order
order in council
ordered
ordering
orderlies
orderly
Orders in Council
ordinal
ordinance
ordinarily
ordinary
ordinary action
ordinary resolution
ordinary shares
ordination
Ordnance Survey
ore
organ
organic
organically
organism
organization
organize
organized
organizing
orgasm
orgies
orgy
orient
oriental

orientate
orientated
orientating
orienteering
orifice
origin
original
originally
originate
originated
originating
originating summons
ornament
ornamental
ornamentally
ornate
orphan
orphanage
orse
orthodox
orthodoxy
orthography
orthopaedic
oscillate
oscillated
oscillating
oscillation
ostensible
ostensible authority
ostensible partner
ostensibly
ostentation
ostentatious
osteopath
ostracism
ostracize
ostracized
ostracizing
other
ought
ounce
our

ours
ourselves
oust
ouster
ouster of jurisdiction
out
outboard
outbreak
outcast
outcome
outcry
outdid
outdo
outdoing
outdone
outdoor
outer
outer Bar
Outer House
outer space
outermost
outfit
outfitter
outing
outlandish
outlaw
outlay
outlet
outline
outlook
outlying
outnumber
outnumbered
outnumbering
out-patient
output
outrage
outrageous
outright
outset
outside
outsize

outskirts
outspoken
outstanding
outward
outwit
outwith
outwitted
outwitting
outwork
oval
ovaries
ovary
ovation
over
overall
overawe
overawed
overawing
overbearing
overcame
overcapacity
overcome
overcoming
overcrowded
overcrowding
overdid
overdo
overdoing
overdone
overdose
overdraft
overdraw
overdrawn
overdue
overflow
overgrown
overheads
overhear
overheard
overhearing
over-insurance
overjoyed

overlap
overlapped
overlapping
overlook
overpowering
overproduction
overran
overrate
overrated
overrating
overreach
overreaching
overriding
overrule
overrun
overrunning
overseas
overseer
overshadow
oversight
oversman
overstep
overstepped
overstepping
over-subscribed
overt
overtake
overtaken
overtaking
overthrew
overthrow
overthrowing
overthrown
overtime
overtook
overture
overwhelm
overwrought
owe
owed
owing
own

owned
owner
owner-occupier
ownership
owning
oxygen
ozone

Pp

pace
paced
pacified
pacifist
pacify
pacifying
pacing
pack
package
packaging
packed
packet
packing
pact
pacta sunt servanda
pactum de non
    petendo
pactum de quota litis
pactum illicitum
pad
padded
padding
paddock
padlock
pagan
page
paged
paging

Pp

pagoda
paid
paid-up capital
pail
pain
pained
painful
painfully
painless
painstaking
paint
painter
painting
pair
paired
pairing
pais
palace
palatable
palate
palatial
pale
palindrome
paling
palisade
pall
palled
pallet
palliative
pallid
palling
pallor
palm
palmist
palmistry
palpable
palpably
palpitation
palsy
paltry
pamper
pampered

pampering
pamphlet
pan
panacea
panache
pandemonium
pander
pandered
pandering
pane
panel
panelling
panic
panicked
panicking
pannage
panned
pannier
panning
panoply
panorama
pantechnicon
pantries
pantry
papacy
papal
paper
papered
papering
par
parable
parachute
parachutist
parade
paraded
parading
paradise
paradox
paradoxes
paradoxical
paradoxically
paraffin

paragon
paragraph
parallel
parallelogram
paralyse
paralysed
paralysing
paralysis
paralytic
parameter
paramount
paramountcy
paramour
parapet
paraphernalia
paraphrase
paraplegia
paraplegic
parasite
parasitic
paratrooper
paratroops
parcel
parcelled
parcelling
parch
parchment
pardon
pardonable
pardoned
pardoning
pare
pared
parens patriae
parent
parent company
parentage
parental
parentheses
parenthesis
parenthetical
pari passu

paring
parish
parishes
parishioner
parity
park
parley
parleyed
parleying
parliament
parliamentary
Parliamentary
  Commissioner for
  Administration
parliamentary counsel
parliamentary election
parliamentary
  privilege
parlour
parochial
parodied
parodies
parody
parodying
parol
parol evidence
parole
parole evidence
paroxysm
parquet
parried
parry
parrying
parse
parsed
parsimonious
parsimony
parsing
parson
parsonage
part
part performance

partake
partaken
partaking
partial
partiality
partially
participant
participate
participated
participating
participation
participle
particle
particular
particular average
particular estate
particular lien
particular tenant
particularly
parties
partisan
partition
partly
partner
partnered
partnering
partnership
partnership at will
partnership by
  estoppel
partook
parts and pertinents
parts, pendicles and
  pertinents
party
party-wall
Pascal
pass
passable
passage
passed
passenger

passer-by
passers-by
passing
passing off
passion
passionate
passionately
passive
passive title
passive trust
passively
passover
passport
password
past
past consideration
paste
pasteurization
pasteurize
pasteurized
pasteurizing
pastime
pastor
pastoral
pasturage
pasture
pat
patch
patches
patchwork
patchy
patent
patent ambiguity
patent defect
patent right
patentee
patently
Patents Court
paternal
paternally
paternity
path

pathetic
pathetically
pathological
pathologist
pathology
pathos
patience
patient
patio
patria potestas
patriarch
patriarchal
patricide
patrimonial
patrimony
patriot
patriotic
patriotically
patriotism
patrol
patrolled
patrolling
patron
patronage
patronize
patronized
patronizing
patted
pattern
patterned
patting
paucity
pauper
pause
paused
pausing
pave
paved
pavement
pavilion
paving
pawn

pawnbroker
pawnee
pawnor
pawn-receipt
pay
pay as you earn
    (PAYE)
payable
payee
paying
payment
payment in due
    course
payroll
pay-slip
peace
peaceable
peaceably
peaceful
peacefully
peak
peal
pealed
pealing
peat
pebble
peculiar
peculiarities
peculiarity
pecuniary
pedant
pedantic
pedantically
peddle
peddled
peddling
pedestal
pedestrian
pedigree
pedigreed
pedlar
pedometer

peer
peerage
peered
peering
peerless
peevish
pejorative
pellet
pelt
pelvis
pen
penal
penal action
penal irritancy
penalize
penalized
penalizing
penalties
penalty
penance
pence
pencil
pencilled
pencilling
pendant
pendens lis
pendent
pendente lite
pending
pendulum
penetrate
penetrated
penetrating
penetration
penicillin
peninsula
penis
penitent
penitentiary
penknife
pennant
penned

pennies
penniless
penning
penny
pension
pensionable
pensioner
pensive
pensively
pentagon
penthouse
pent-up
penultimate
penury
people
peopled
peopling
peppercorn rent
per annum
per autre vie
per capita
per cent
per cur
per curiam
per incuriam
per infortunium
per minas
per my et per tout
per pais
per pro
per procurationem pp
per quod
per se
per stirpes
per subsequens
  matrimonium
perceive
perceived
perceiving
percentage
perceptible
perceptibly

perception
perceptive
percolate
percolated
percolating
perdition
peremptorily
peremptory
peremptory pleas
perennial
perennially
perfect
perfect right
perfection
perfectionist
perfidious
perfidy
perforate
perforated
perforating
perform
performance
performance bond
performer
perfunctorily
perfunctory
perhaps
periculo petentis
peril
perilous
perimeter
period
periodic
periodic tenancy
periodical
periodical allowance
periodically
peripatetic
peripheral
peripheries
periphery
periscope

perish
perishable
perished
perjure
perjured
perjuring
perjury
permanence
permanency
permanent
permeable
permeate
permeated
permeating
permissible
permission
permissive
permissive waste
permissiveness
permit
permitted
permitted
  development
permitting
permutation
pernicious
perpendicular
perpetrate
perpetrated
perpetrating
perpetrator
perpetual
perpetually
perpetuate
perpetuated
perpetuating
perpetuating
  testimony
perpetuity
perplex
perplexities
perplexity

perquisite
persecute
persecuted
persecuting
persecution
persecutor
perseverance
persevere
persevered
persevering
persist
persistence
persistent
person
person under disability
persona non grata
persona standi in
  judicio
personable
personal
personal bar
personal estate
personal exception
personal property
personal right
personal security
personal servitude
personalities
personality
personally
personalty
personation
personification
personified
personify
personifying
personnel
perspective
Perspex®
perspicacious
perspicacity
persuade

persuaded
persuading
persuasion
persuasive
persuasive authorities
persuasively
pertain
pertained
pertaining
pertinacious
pertinacity
pertinence
pertinent
pertinents
perturb
perturbation
perusal
peruse
perused
perusing
pervade
pervaded
pervading
perverse
perverse verdict
perversely
perversion
perversity
pervert
perverting the course
  of justice
peseta
pessimism
pessimist
pessimistic
pessimistically
pest
pester
pestered
pestering
pesticide
pestilence

pet
peter out
petered out
petering out
petition
petition and complaint
petitioner
petitory action
petrified
petrify
petrifying
petrol
petroleum
petted
pettily
pettiness
petting
petty
petty assize
petty jury
petty sessions
petulance
petulant
pew
pewter
phantom
pharmaceutical
pharmacies
pharmacist
pharmacological
pharmacologist
pharmacology
pharmacy
pharyngitis
pharynx
phase
phased
phasing
phenomena
phenomenal
phenomenon
phial

philander
philandered
philanderer
philandering
philanthropic
philanthropically
philanthropist
philanthropy
philatelist
philately
philosopher
philosophic
philosophically
philosophy
phlegm
phlegmatic
phobia
phobic
phone
phonetics
phosphate
phosphorescent
phosphorous
photocopied
photocopy
photocopying
photogenic
photogenically
photograph
photographer
photographic
photographically
photography
phrase
phrased
phraseology
phrasing
physical
physically
physician
physicist
physics

physiological
physiologically
physiologist
physiology
physiotherapist
physiotherapy
physique
pick
picket
picketed
picketing
pick-pocket
pictorial
pictorially
picture
picturesque
picturesquely
piece
piecemeal
piecework
pied-à-terre
pier
pierce
pierced
piercing
piety
pig
pigeon
pigeon-hole
piggery
pigment
pigmentation
pigsty
pile
piled
pilfer
pilfered
pilfering
pilgrim
pilgrimage
piling
pill

pillage
pillar
pillion
pilloried
pillories
pillory
pillorying
pillow
pilot
piloted
piloting
pin
pince-nez
pincers
pinch
pinched
pinches
pine
pined
pining
pinion
pinioned
pinioning
pinnacle
pinned
pinning
pint
pioneer
pioneered
pioneering
pious
pipe
piped
pipeline
piper
pipette
piping
pique
piqued
piquing
piracy
pirate

piscary
pistol
piston
pit
pitch
pitcher
pitches
piteous
pitfall
pith
pithy
pitiable
pitied
pitiful
pitifully
pittance
pitted
pitting
pity
pitying
pivot
pivoted
pivoting
placard
placate
placated
placating
place
placed
places
placid
placing
plagiarism
plagiarize
plagiarized
plagiarizing
plagium
plague
plaid
plain
plaint
plaintiff

plaintive
plait
plaited
plaiting
plan
plane
planet
planetary
plank
plankton
planned
planning
planning permission
plant
plantation
planter
plaque
plasma
plaster
plastered
plasterer
plastering
plastic
plasticity
plate
plateau
plateaus
plateaux
plated
platform
plating
platinum
platitude
platonic
platoon
platter
plaudit
plausibility
plausible
plausibly
play
played

player
playing
playwright
plea
plea bargaining
plea in bar
plea-in-law
plea in mitigation
plead
pleading
pleas of the crown
pleasant
pleasantness
pleasantries
pleasantry
please
pleased
pleasing
pleasurable
pleasurably
pleasure
plebeian
plebiscite
pledge
pledged
pledgee
pledging
pledgor
plenary
plene administravit
plenipotentiary
plenteous
plentiful
plentifully
plenty
plethora
pleurisy
pliable
pliant
plied
pliers
plight

plimsoll
plod
plodded
plodding
plot
plotted
plotting
plough
plough bote
ploughed
ploughing
pluck
pluckily
plucky
plug
plugged
plugging
plumb
plumbed
plumber
plumbing
plumbline
plume
plummet
plump
plunder
plundered
plundering
plunge
plunged
plunging
plural
plurality
pluris petitio
plus
plutocrat
plutocratic
ply
plying
pneumatic
pneumatically
pneumonia

poach
poacher
poaching
pocket
pocketed
pocketing
pockmark
pod
poignance
poignant
poind
poinding
poinding of the ground
point
point of law
pointed
pointer
pointless
poise
poised
poison
poison pill
poisonous
poke
poked
poker
poking
polar
pole
police
Police Complaints
    Authority
police detention
policed
policeman
policemen
policies
policing
policy
polio
poliomyelitis
polite

politely
politeness
politic
political
political asylum
politically
politician
politics
poll
poll tax
polled
polling
pollute
polluted
polluting
pollution
poltergeist
polygamist
polygamous
polygamy
polyglot
polygon
polysyllabic
polytechnic
polythene
pomp
pompous
pond
ponder
pondered
pondering
ponderous
pontiff
pontificate
pontificated
pontificating
pontoon
pool
pooled
pooling
poor
poorly

pope
populace
popular
popularity
popularize
popularized
popularizing
populate
populated
populating
population
populous
porcelain
porch
porches
pore
pored
poring
pornographic
pornography
porous
port
portable
portal
portcullis
portcullises
portend
portent
portentous
porter
portfolio
port-hole
portico
porticoes
porticos
portion
portion-debt
portioner
portly
portmanteau
portmanteaus
portmanteaux

portrait
portray
portrayal
portrayed
portraying
Portuguese
pose
posed
poser
poseur
posing
position
positioned
positioning
positive
positively
possess
possessed
possessing
possession
possessive
possessively
possessor
possessory action
possessory lien
possessory title
possibilities
possibility
possible
possibly
post
post diem
post hoc ergo propter
    hoc
post litem motam
postage
postal
postal divorce
postcard
post-dated
post-dated cheque
poste restante

poster
posterior
posterity
postern
posthumous
postive prescription
postmortem
postpone
postponed
postponed claim
postponement
postponing
postscript
postulate
postulated
postulating
potash
potassium
potency
potent
potential
potentially
pothole
potholing
potior est conditio
    defendentis
potior est conditio
    possidentis
pouch
pouches
poultice
poultry
pounce
pounced
pouncing
pound
pour
poured
pouring
poverty
powder
powdered

powdering
powdery
power
power of appointment
power of attorney
powered
powerful
powerfully
powerless
practicable
practical
practically
practice
practise
practised
practising
practising certificate
practitioner
praedial servitude
praepositura
pragmatic
pragmatist
praise
praised
praising
pray
prayed
prayer
praying
preach
preacher
preamble
prearrange
prearranged
prearranging
precario
precarious
precarious possession
precatory
precaution
precautionary
precede

preceded
precedence
precedent
preceding
precept
precept of arrestment
precept of clare
    constat
precept of poinding
precept of sasine
precept of warning
precinct
precious
precipice
precipitate
precipitated
precipitating
precipitous
précis
precise
precisely
precision
preclude
precluded
precluding
precocious
precocity
precognition
precognosce
preconception
precursor
predator
predatory
predecessor
predecessor in title
predicament
predict
predictable
predictably
prediction
predilection
predominant

pre-eminent
pre-emption
pre-emptive
prefabricated
preface
prefect
prefer
preferable
preference
preference shares
preferential
preferential claim
preferential debts
preferment
preferred
preferring
prefix
prefixes
pregnancies
pregnancy
pregnant
prehistoric
prehistorically
prejudge
prejudged
prejudging
prejudice
prejudiced
prejudicial
prejudicing
prelate
preliminaries
preliminary
preliminary defences
prelude
premature
prematurely
premeditated
premier
première
premise
premises

premium
premonition
preoccupation
preoccupied
prepaid
preparation
preparatory
prepare
prepared
preparing
prepay
prepaying
prepayment
preponderance
preposition
prepossessing
preposterous
prerequisite
prerogative
prerogative of mercy
presage
presaged
presaging
Presbyterian
presbytery
prescribe
prescribed
prescribing
prescription
prescriptive
prescriptive period
presence
present
presentable
presentably
presentation
presentiment
presently
presentment
preservation
preservation of
    amenity

preservative
preserve
preserved
preserving
preses
preside
presided
presidency
president
President of the
    Family Division (P)
presiding
press
pressgang
pressure
pressurize
pressurized
pressurizing
prestable
prestation
Prestel®
prestige
prestigious
presumably
presume
presumed
presuming
presumption
presumption of death
presumption of
    innocence
presumptuous
pretence
pretend
pretender
pretension
pretentious
preternatural
preternaturally
pretext
pretium affectionis
prettily

prettiness
pretty
prevail
prevailed
prevailing
prevalence
prevalent
prevaricate
prevaricated
prevaricating
prevarication
prevent
preventive
preview
previous
previously
prey
preyed
preying
price
priced
priceless
pricing
pride
prided
priding
pried
priest
priesthood
priggish
prim
prima donna
prima facie
primarily
primary
primate
prime
Prime Minister
primed
primer
primeval
priming

primitive
primitively
primo loco
primogeniture
prince
princess
princesses
principal
principal security
principalities
principality
principally
principle
print
printer
prior
prior rights
priorities
priority
prise
prised
prising
prism
prison
prisoner
pristine
privacy
private
private carrier
private company
private jurisdiction
private nuisance
privateer
privately
privation
privatization
privilege
privileged
privileged claim
privileged debts
privileged summons
privity

privy
Privy Council (PC)
prize
prized
prizing
pro bono publico
pro confesso
pro forma
pro indiviso
pro loco et tempore
pro non scripto
pro rata
pro re nata
pro tanto
pro veritate
probabilis causa
  litigandi
probabilities
probability
probable
probably
probate
probatio probata
probation
probation officer
probationer
probative
probative document
probe
probed
probing
probity
problem
problematic
procedendo
procedure
procedure roll
proceed
proceeded
proceeding
process
process caption

processed
processes
processing
procession
proclaim
proclamation
procrastinate
procrastinated
procrastinating
procrastination
procreation
procurator
procurator fiscal
procuratory
procure
procured
procurement
procuring
prod
prodded
prodding
prodigal
prodigies
prodigious
prodigy
produce
produced
producer
producing
product
product liability
production
productive
productively
productivity
profane
profanely
profanity
profess
profession
professional
professionally

Pp

professor
proffer
proffered
proffering
proficiency
proficient
profile
profit
profit and loss account
profitable
profitably
profited
profiteer
profiteered
profiteering
profiting
profits
profits à prendre
profit-sharing
profligacy
profligate
pro-forma invoice
profound
profuse
profusely
profusion
progenitor
progeny
prognosticate
prognosticated
prognosticating
prognostication
program
programmable
programme
programmed
programming
progress
progress of titles
progression
progressive
progressively

prohibit
prohibited
prohibiting
prohibition
prohibitive
prohibitively
project
projectile
projection
projector
proletarian
proletariat
proliferate
proliferated
proliferating
prolific
prolixity
prologue
prolong
promenade
prominence
prominent
promiscuity
promiscuous
promise
promised
promises
promising
promissory estoppel
promissory note
promontories
promontory
promote
promoted
promoter
promoting
promotion
prompt
promptly
prone
pronoun
pronounce

pronounced
pronouncement
pronouncing
pronunciation
proof
proof before answer
proof in replication
prop
propaganda
propagandist
propagate
propagated
propagating
propagator
propel
propelled
propeller
propelling
propensities
propensity
proper
properly
properties
property
property in goods
prophecies
prophecy
prophesied
prophesy
prophesying
prophet
propinquity
propitiate
propitiated
propitiating
propone
proponent
proportion
proportional
proportionality
proportionally
proportionate

proportionately
proposal
propose
proposed
proposing
proposition
propositus
propound
propped
propping
proprietary
proprietary estoppel
proprieties
proprietor
proprietorship
proprietory
proprietress
proprietrix
propriety
propulsion
prorogate
prorogation
prorogue
prosaic
prosaically
proscribe
proscribed
prose
prosecute
prosecuted
prosecuting
prosecution
prosecutor
prospect
prospective
prospector
prospectus
prospectuses
prosper
prospered
prospering
prosperity

prosperous
prostate
prostitute
prostitution
prostrate
prostrated
prostrating
prostration
protagonist
protect
protected
protected tenancy
protection
protectionism
protective
protectively
protector
protégé
protein
protest
Protestant
protestation
protocol
proton
prototype
protract
protractor
protrude
protruded
protruding
protrusion
protuberance
protuberant
proud
prout de jure
prove
proved
provender
proverb
proverbial
proverbially
provide

provided
providence
provident
providential
providentially
providing
province
provincial
provincially
proving
proving a debt
proving a will
proving the tenor
provision
provisional
provisionally
proviso
provocation
provocative
provocatively
provoke
provoked
provoking
provost
prowess
prowl
prowler
proxies
proximity
proxy
prude
prudence
prudent
prudery
prudish
pry
prying
pseudo
pseudonym
psychiatric
psychiatrist
psychiatry

psychic
psychoanalysis
psychological
psychologically
psychologist
psychology
psychopath
psychopathic
psychoses
psychosis
puberty
pubic
public
public burdens
public company
public limited
  company (plc)
public nuisance
public roup
publican
publication
publicity
publicly
publish
publisher
puddle
puerile
puff
pugilist
pugnacious
pugnacity
puisne
pull
pulley
pulmonary
pulpit
pulse
pulverize
pulverized
pulverizing
pummel
pummelled

pummelling
pump
pun
punch
punches
punctilious
punctual
punctuality
punctually
punctuate
punctuated
punctuating
punctuation
puncture
punctured
puncturing
pundit
pungent
punish
punishable
punishment
punitive
punned
punning
puny
pupil
pupillage
pupillarity
purchase
purchased
purchaser
purchasing
pure
purely
purgation
purgative
purgatory
purge
purged
purging
purification
purified

purify
purifying
purist
puritan
puritanical
puritanically
purity
purloin
purport
purpose
purposeful
purposefully
purposely
purse
purser
pursue
pursued
pursuer
pursuing
pursuit
put
putative
putative father
putrefaction
putrefy
putrefying
putrid
putrified
putting
puzzle
puzzled
puzzling
pylon
pyramid
pyramid selling
pyre

Qq

qua
quad
quadrangle
quadrangular
quadrant
quadriennium utile
quadrilateral
quadruped
quadruple
quaint
qualification
qualified
qualified acceptance
qualified privilege
qualified title
qualify
qualifying
qualifying capital
  interest
qualitative
qualities
quality
qualm
quam primum
quamdiu se bene
  gesserit
quandaries
quandary
quango
quanti minoris
quantitative
quantities
quantity
quantum
quantum lucratus
quantum meruit
quantum valeat
quantum valebat

quarantine
quarrel
quarrelled
quarrelling
quarrelsome
quarried
quarries
quarry
quarrying
quart
quarter
quarter days
quarterly
quartet
quartz
quash
quasi
quasi-contract
quasi-delict
quasi-easements
quasi-entail
quasi ex contractu
quasi-judicial
quasi-negotiable
  instrument
quaver
quavered
quavering
quay
queasily
queasiness
queasy
queen
Queen's and Lord
  Treasurer's
  Remembrancer
Queen's Bench (QB)
Queen's Bench
  Division (QBD)
Queen's Counsel
  (QC)
Queen's Proctor

Queen's Signet
Queen's
  Remembrancer
queer
quell
quench
queried
queries
querulous
query
querying
quest
question
questionable
questionably
questioned
questioning
questionnaire
queue
queued
queueing
queuing
qui approbat non
  reprobat
qui facit per alium facit
  per se
qui prior est tempore
  potior est jure
qui sentit commodum
  sentire debet et
  onus; et e contra
quia timet
quibble
quibbled
quibbling
quick
quicken
quickened
quickening
quickness
quicquid plantatur
  solo, solo cedit

quid juris
quid pro quo
quiescent
quiet
quiet enjoyment
quiet possession
quieten
quietened
quietening
quietness
quill
quin
quinine
quinquennial
quinquennial
  prescription
quintessence
quintessential
quintet
quintuplet
quip
quipped
quipping
quire
quirering
quirk
quit
quit rent
quite
quitted
quitting
quiver
quivered
quixotic
quixotically
quiz
quizzed
quizzes
quizzical
quizzically
quizzing
quo jure

quoad ultra
quorum
quota
quotation
quote
quoted
quoted company
quotient
quoting

Rr

rabbi
rabble
rabid
rabies
race
racecourse
racial
racial discrimination
racialism
racialist
racially
racism
racist
rack
rack rent
racket
racketeer
raconteur
racy
radar
radar trap
radiance
radiant
radiate
radiated

radiating
radiation
radiator
radical
radically
radii
radio
radioactive
radioed
radioing
radiologist
radiology
radiotherapist
radiotherapy
radium
radius
rafter
rage
raged
raging
raid
raider
rail
railing
railway
raiment
rain
rained
raining
raise
raised
raising
rallied
rallies
rally
rallying
ram
Ramadan
ramification
rammed
ramming
ramp

rampage
rampaged
rampaging
rampant
ran
ranch
ranches
rancorous
rancour
rand
random
rang
range
ranged
ranger
ranging
rank
rankle
rankled
rankling
ransack
ransom
ransomed
ransoming
rant
rap
rapacious
rape
raped
rapid
rapidity
rapier
raping
rapped
rapping
rare
rarefied
rarely
raring
rarities
rarity
rascal

rascally
rash
rashness
rasp
Rastafarian
rat
ratchet
rate
rateable
rateable value
rated
rather
ratification
ratified
ratify
ratifying
rating
ratio
ratio decidendi
ration
rational
rationalization
rationalize
rationalized
rationalizing
rationally
rationed
rationing
ratted
ratting
raucous
ravage
ravaged
ravaging
rave
raved
ravenous
ravine
raving
ray
raze
razed

razing
razor
re
re mercatoria
reach
react
reaction
reactionary
read
reader
readily
readiness
reading
ready
real
real action
real burden
real estate
real evidence
real raiser
real right
real security
real warrandice
realism
realist
realistic
realistically
realities
reality
realization
realize
realized
realizing
really
realm
realty
ream
reap
reaped
reaper
reaping
rear

reared
rearguard
rearing
reason
reasonable
reasonable repair
reasonably
reasoned
reasoning
reassurance
reassure
reassured
reassuring
rebate
rebel
rebelled
rebelling
rebellion
rebellious
rebound
rebuff
rebuke
rebuked
rebuking
rebus sic stantibus
rebut
rebuttable
  presumption
rebuttal
rebutted
rebutter
rebutting
recalcitrance
recalcitrant
recall
recalled
recalling
recant
recap
recapitulate
recapitulated
recapitulating

recapitulation
recapped
recapping
recaption
recapture
recaptured
recapturing
recede
receded
receding
receipt
receive
received
receiver
receiving
recent
recent possession
recently
receptacle
reception
receptionist
receptive
recess
recesses
recession
recipient
reciprocal
reciprocally
reciprocate
reciprocated
reciprocating
recital
recitation
recite
recited
reciting
reckless
reckless driving
recklessness
reckon
reckoned
reckoning

reclaim
reclaiming motion
reclamation
recline
reclined
reclining
recluse
recognisance
recognition
recognizable
recognizably
recognize
recognized
recognizing
recoil
recoiled
recoiling
recollect
recollection
recommend
recommendation
recompense
reconcile
reconciled
reconciliation
reconciling
recondite
reconnaissance
reconnoitre
reconnoitred
reconnoitring
reconstruction
reconvention
reconversion
reconvey
reconveyance
record
recorded
recorder
Recorder
recording
recount

recoup
recouped
recouping
recourse
recover
recovered
recovering
recovery
recreation
recreational charity
recrimination
recruit
recruited
recruiting
recruitment
rectangle
rectangular
rectification
rectified
rectify
rectifying
rectitude
rector
rectories
rectory
rectum
recumbent
recuperate
recuperated
recuperating
recuperation
recuperative
recur
recurred
recurrence
recurrent
recurring
reddendo
reddendum
redeem
redeem up, foreclose
  down

redeemable
redeemable
  preference shares
Redeemer
redeeming
redemption
redeploy
redeployed
redeploying
red-handed
redolent
redouble
redoubled
redoubling
redoubtable
redress
reduce
reduced
reducing
reduction
redundancies
redundancy
redundant
reek
reel
reeled
reeling
re-engage
re-engagement
re-entry
re-examination
refectories
refectory
refer
refer to drawer
referee
reference
referenda
referendum
referendums
referential
referred

referring
refine
refined
refinement
refineries
refinery
refining
reflation
reflect
reflection
reflective
reflectively
reflector
reflex
reflexive
reform
reformation
reformer
refraction
refractory
refrain
refrained
refraining
refresh
refreshing
refuel
refuelled
refuelling
refuge
refugee
refund
refusal
refuse
refused
refusing
refute
refuted
refuting
regain
regained
regaining
regalia

Rr

regalia majora
regalia minora
regard
regarding
regardless
regeneration
regent
regiam majestatem
régime
regiment
regimental
regimentation
Regina
region
regional
regional assessor
regionally
register
register of directors
register of directors'
 interests
Register of Inhibitions
 and Adjudications
Register of Sasines
registered
registered design
registered land
registered office
registering
registrar
registration
registration for
 execution
registration for
 preservation
registration for
 publication
registration of title
registries
registry
regret
regretful

regretfully
regrettable
regrettably
regretted
regretting
regular
regularity
regulate
regulated
regulating
regulation
regulator
rehabilitate
rehabilitated
rehabilitating
rehabilitation
re-hearing
rehearse
rehearsed
rehearsing
rei interitus
rei interventus
reimburse
reimbursed
reimbursing
reincarnation
reinforce
reinforced
reinforcements
reinforcing
reinstate
reinstated
reinstatement
reinstating
reinsurance
reinsure
reinsured
reinsurer
reiterate
reiterated
reiterating
reiteration

reiterative
reject
rejected
rejection
rejoinder
rejuvenate
rejuvenated
rejuvenating
relagating
relapse
relapsed
relapsing
relate
related
relating
relation
relationship
relative
relatively
relator
relax
relaxation
relay
relayed
relaying
release
released
releasing
relegate
relegated
relegation
relent
relentless
relevance
relevancy
relevant
relevant evidence
relevant facts
reliable
reliably
reliance
reliant

relic
relict
relied
relief
relieve
relieved
relieving
religion
religious
relinquish
relish
relocation
reluctance
reluctant
rely
relying
remain
remainder
remainderman
remained
remaining
remand
remark
remarkable
remarkably
remedial
remedial rights
remedied
remedies
remedy
remedying
remember
remembered
remembering
remembrance
remind
reminder
reminisce
reminisced
reminiscence
reminiscent
reminiscing

remise
remiss
remissio injuriae
remission
remit
remittance
remitted
remitting
remnant
remonstrance
remonstrate
remonstrated
remonstrating
remorse
remorseful
remorsefully
remorseless
remote
remotely
remoteness
removal
remove
removed
removing
remunerate
remunerated
remunerating
remuneration
remunerative
renal
render
rendered
rendering
rendezvous
renegade
renew
renewal
renounce
renounced
renouncing
renovate
renovated

renovating
renovation
renown
renowned
rent
rent rebate
rent service
rental
rentaller
rentcharge
rentier
renunciation
renvoi
reorganization
reorganize
reorganized
reorganizing
repaid
repair
repaired
repairing
reparation
repartee
repatriate
repatriated
repatriating
repatriation
repay
repaying
repayment
repeal
repealed
repealing
repeat
repeated
repeatedly
repeating
repel
repellant
repelled
repellent
repelling

repent
repentance
repentant
repercussion
repertoire
repetition
repetitious
repetitive
repetitively
replace
replaced
replacement
replacing
replenish
replete
replevin
replica
replied
replies
reply
replying
repone
report
reporter
reporter to the
children's panel
repose
repositories
repository
re-possess
re-possession
reprehensible
reprehensibly
represent
representation
representative
represented
repress
repression
repressive
reprieve
reprieved

reprieving
reprimand
reprisal
reproach
reproaches
reproachful
reproachfully
reprobate
reproduce
reproduced
reproducing
reproduction
reproof
reprove
reproved
reproving
republic
republican
republication
republish
repudiate
repudiated
repudiating
repudiation
repugnance
repugnancy
repugnant
repulsive
repulsively
reputable
reputation
repute
reputed
reputedly
request
requesting court
requiem
require
required
requirement
requiring
requisite

requisition
reregistration
res
res communes
res extincta
res furtivae
res gestae
res integra
res inter alios acta
res inter alios acta
alteri nocere non
debet
res ipsa loquitur
res judicata
res merae facultatis
res mercatoria
res nova
res noviter veniens ad
notitiam
res nullius
res perit
res perit domino
res publicae
res sua
res universitatis
resale
rescind
rescission
rescous
rescue
rescued
rescuing
resealing
research
researcher
researches
resemblance
resemble
resembled
resembling
resent
resentful

resentfully
resentment
reservation
reserve
reserve capital
reserved
reserving
reservoir
reset
reset of theft
reside
resided
residence
resident
residential
residing
residual
residuary devise
residuary devisee
residuary estate
residuary legacy
residuary legatee
residue
resign
resignation
resigned
resigning
resile
resilience
resilient
resist
resistance
resisting arrest
resolute
resolutely
resolution
resolutive
resolve
resolved
resolving
resonance
resonant

resonate
resonated
resonating
resort
resounding
resource
resourceful
respect
respectability
respectable
respectably
respectful
respectfully
respective
respectively
respiration
respirator
respite
resplendent
respond
respondeat superior
respondent
response
responsibilities
responsibility
responsible
responsibly
responsive
rest
restaurant
restaurateur
restful
restfully
resting-owing
restitutio in integrum
restitution
restive
restively
restless
restoration
restore
restored

restoring
restrain
restrained
restraining
restraint
restraint of marriage
restraint of trade
restraints of princes
restrict
restricted contract
restriction
restrictive
restrictive covenant
restrictive
    endorsement
Restrictive Practices
    Court
restrictive trade
    practices
result
resultant
resulting trust
resulting use
resume
résumé
resumed
resuming
resumption
resurgence
resurgent
resurrect
resurrection
resuscitate
resuscitated
resuscitating
resuscitation
retail
retailed
retailer
retailing
retain
retained

retainer
retaining
retaliate
retaliated
retaliating
retaliation
retarded
retention
retentive
reticence
reticent
retina
retinae
retinas
retiral
retire
retired
retirement
retiring
retort
retour sans protêt
retrace
retraced
retracing
retract
retractable
retraction
retreat
retreated
retreating
retrial
retribution
retributive justice
retrieve
retrieved
retriever
retrieving
retroactive legislation
retrocession
retrograde
retrospect
retrospective

retrospective
  legislation
retrospectively
return
returnable
returning officer
reunion
reunite
reunited
reuniting
revaluation
reveal
revealed
revealing
revel
revelation
revelled
reveller
revelling
revelry
revenge
revenged
revenging
revenue
reverberate
reverberated
reverberating
reverberation
revere
revered
reverence
Reverend
reverent
reverential
reverentially
reverie
revering
reversal
reverse
reversed
reversible
reversing

reversion
reversionary
reversionary interest
revert
reverter
review
reviewer
revile
reviled
reviling
revise
revised
revising
revision
revival
revive
revived
reviving
revocation
revoke
revoked
revoking
revolt
revolting
revolution
revolutionaries
revolutionary
revolutionize
revolutionized
revolutionizing
revolve
revolved
revolver
revolving
revulsion
reward
Rex
rhetoric
rhetorical
rhetorically
rheumatic
rheumatism

rhythm
rhythmic
rhythmical
rhythmically
rib
ribald
rich
riches
richness
rickets
rickety
ricochet
ricocheted
ricocheting
rid
riddance
ridden
ridding
riddle
riddled
riddling
ride
rider
ridge
ridicule
ridiculed
ridiculing
ridiculous
riding
riding claim
riding interest
rife
rifle
rifled
rifling
rift
rig
rigged
rigging
right
right ex lege
right of action

right of audience
right of entry
right of support
right of way
righteous
righteousness
rightful
rightfully
rights issue
rights offer
rigid
rigmarole
rigorous
rigour
rim
ring
ringing
riot
rioted
rioter
rioting
riotous
rip
riparian
ripped
ripping
rise
risen
rising
risk
risky
rite
ritual
ritually
river
rivet
riveted
riveting
road
roam
roamed
roaming

roar
roared
roaring
rob
robbed
robberies
robbery
robbing
robe
robot
robust
rock
rocky
rode
rodent
rogatory
rogue
roguish
rôle
roll
rolled-up plea
rolls
Romalpa clause
Roman
romance
Romanian
romantic
romantically
roof
roomy
root
root of contract
root of title
rooted
rooting
rope
roped
roping
rosaries
rosary
rose
rosette

roster
rostra
rostrum
rostrums
rot
rota
rotary
rotate
rotated
rotating
rotation
rote
rotted
rotten
rotting
rotund
rough
roughen
roughened
roughening
roulette
round
rounders
roup
roup and sale
rouse
roused
rousing
rout
route
routine
routinely
row
rowdy
rowdyism
royal
royal assent
royal prerogative
royal warrant
royalist
royally
royalties

royalty
rub
rubbed
rubber
rubbing
rubbish
rubble
rubies
rubric
ruby
rucksack
rudder
rude
rudely
rudeness
rudimentary
rudiments
rue
rued
rueful
ruefully
ruffian
Rugby
ruin
ruination
ruined
ruing
ruining
ruinous
ruinously
rule
rule of law
ruled
ruler
rules of court
Rules of the Supreme
    Court (RSC)
ruling
Rumanian
ruminant
ruminate
ruminated

ruminating
rummage
rummaged
rummaging
rumour
run
rune
rung
runner
runner-up
running
running days
running with the land
runway
rupee
rupture
ruptured
rupturing
rural
ruse
rush
Russian
rust
rustler
rusty
rut
ruthless
ruthlessness
rutted
rutting

Ss

Sabbath
sabotage
saboteur

sack
sacrament
sacred
sacrifice
sacrificed
sacrificial
sacrificing
sacrilege
sacrilegious
sacrosanct
sad
sadden
saddened
saddening
sadder
saddest
sadism
sadist
sadistic
sadistically
sadly
sadness
safe
safe goods
safe port
safeguard
safely
safety
sag
saga
sagacious
sagacity
sage
sagely
sagged
sagging
said
sail
sailed
sailing
sailor
saint

saintly
salaries
salary
sale
sale by description
sale of goods
sale or return
salesman
salient
saline
saliva
salivary
salivate
salivated
salivating
sallied
sallies
sallow
sally
sallying
saloon
salubrious
salutary
salutation
salute
saluted
saluting
salvage
salvaged
salvaging
salvation
salve
salved
salver
salving
salvo
salvoes
salvor
same
sameness
sample
sampled

sampling
sanatoria
sanatorium
sanatoriums
sanctified
sanctify
sanctifying
sanctimonious
sanction
sanctioned
sanctioning
sanctity
sanctuaries
sanctuary
sane
sanely
saneness
sang
sanguine
sanguinely
sanitary
sanitation
sanity
sank
sans recours
sap
sapling
sapped
sapphire
sapping
sarcasm
sarcastic
sarcastically
sarcophagi
sarcophagus
sarcophaguses
sardonic
sardonically
sartorial
sash
sashes
sasine

sat	sawn	sceptic
Satan	saxophone	sceptical
satanic	say	sceptically
sated	saying	scepticism
satellite	scabies	schedule
satiate	scaffold	scheme
satiated	scaffolding	schemed
satiating	scald	scheming
satiety	scale	schism
satire	scalp	schizophrenia
satirical	scalpel	schizophrenic
satirically	scaly	scholar
satirist	scan	scholarly
satisfaction	scandal	scholarship
satisfactorily	scandalize	scholastic
satisfactory	scandalized	scholastically
satisfied	scandalizing	school
satisfied term	scandalmonger	schooled
satisfy	scandalous	schoolfellow
satisfying	scanned	schooling
saturate	scanning	schooner
saturated	scansion	sciatica
saturating	scant	science
saturation	scantily	scienter
Saturday	scanty	scientific
saturnine	scapegoat	scientifically
saunter	scar	scientist
sauntered	scarce	scil
sauntering	scarcely	scilicet
savage	scarcities	scintillate
savagely	scarcity	scintillated
savagery	scare	scintillating
save	scared	scissors
saved	scaring	scoff
saving	scarred	scold
savings bank	scarring	scolding
saviour	scathing	scoop
savoir faire	scatter	scooped
savour	scattered	scooping
saw	scattering	scope
sawed	scavenger	scorch
sawing	scene	score

scored
scorer
scoring
scorn
scornful
scornfully
Scottish Land Court
Scottish Office
scour
scoured
scourge
scourged
scourging
scouring
scout
scowl
scramble
scrambled
scrambling
scrap
scrape
scraped
scraping
scrapped
scrapping
scratch
scratches
scrawl
scream
screamed
screaming
scree
screed
screen
screw
screwed
screwing
scribble
scribbled
scribbling
scrip
scrip issue

scripture
scroll
scrub
scrubbed
scrubbing
scruff
scruple
scrupulous
scrupulously
scrutinize
scrutinized
scrutinizing
scrutiny
scuffle
sculleries
scullery
sculptor
sculpture
scum
scupper
scuppered
scuppering
scurried
scurrilous
scurry
scurrying
scurvy
scuttle
scuttled
scuttling
scythe
se defendendo
sea
seal
sealed
sealing
seam
seamy
séance
sear
search
search and seizure

search for
   encumbrances
search for
   incumbrances
search warrant
searches
seared
searing
seashore
season
seasonable
seasonal
seasonally
seasoned
seasoning
seat
seated
seating
seaworthy
secede
seceded
seceding
secession
secluded
seclusion
second
secondary
secondary creditor
secondary evidence of
   document
secondary party
secondary use
secrecy
secret
secret profits
secret reserves
secret trust
secretarial
secretaries
secretary
Secretary of State
secrete

secreted
secreting
secretion
secretive
secretively
sect
sectarian
section
sector
secular
secundum legem
secure
secure tenancy
secured
secured creditor
securely
securing
securities
security
secus
sed quaere
sedate
sedately
sedation
sedative
sedentary
sederunt
sediment
sedition
seditious
seditious libel
seduce
seduced
seducing
seduction
seductive
seductively
see
seed
seeing
seek
seeking

seem
seemed
seeming
seemingly
seemly
seen
seep
seeped
seeping
seethe
seethed
seething
segment
segregate
segregated
segregating
segregation
seignory
seised
seisin
seisin in deed
seisin in law
seismic
seize
seized
seizing
seizure
seldom
select
select committee
selection
selective
self
self-dealing
self-defence
self-employed
self-help
selfish
sell
seller
selling
selves

semblance
semble
seminar
senate
senator
Senator of the College
    of Justice
send
sending
senile
senility
senior
senior counsel
seniority
sensation
sensational
sensationally
sense
sensed
senseless
sensible
sensibly
sensing
sensitive
sensitively
sensitivity
sensory
sensual
sensually
sensuous
sent
sentence
sentenced
sentencing
sentimental
sentimentality
sentimentally
sentinel
separate
separate counts
separated
separately

separatim
separating
separation
separation of powers
September
septic
septuagenarian
sepulchral
sepulchre
sequel
sequence
sequestered
sequestrate
sequestration
sequestrator
seraphic
sere
serenade
serene
serenely
serenity
serf
serge
sergeant
seriatim
series
serious
Serious Fraud Office
sermon
serrated
serried
serum
servant
serve
served
service
service director
service of heir
serviceable
servient tenement
serviette
servile

servilely
servility
serving
servitude
session
set
set-off
setting
setting aside
setting down
settle
settled
settlement
settler
settling
settling-day
settlor
seven
seventeen
seventeenth
seventh
seventieth
seventy
sever
several
several fishery
several tenancy
severalty
severance
severe
severed
severely
severing
severity
sewage
sewer
sex
sex discrimination
sexagenarian
sexual
sexual deviancy
sexual harassment

sexual intercourse
sexually
shabbily
shabby
shackles
shade
shaded
shading
shadow
shadow director
shady
shaft
shake
shaken
shakily
shaking
shaky
shall
shallow
sham
sham company
sham marriage
sham plea
shambles
shame
shamed
shameful
shamefully
shameless
shaming
shammed
shamming
shape
shaped
shapeless
shapely
shaping
share
share capital
share certificate
share transfer
shared

shareholder
sharing
shark-repellent
sharp
sharpen
sharpened
sharpener
sharpening
shatter
shattered
shattering
shave
shaved
shaving
sheaf
sheath
sheaves
shed
sheer
sheered
sheering
sheet
shelter
sheltered
sheltering
shelve
sheriff
sheriff clerk
sheriff court
sheriff court
  proceedings
sheriff officer
sheriff principal
shewer
shied
shield
shier
shiest
shift
shiftily
shiftless
shifty

shilling
shin
ship
ship-broker
shipped
shipping
shipwreck
shire
shirk
shirker
shock
shocking
shoddily
shoddy
shook
shoot
shooting
shop
shop steward
shop-lifting
shore
short
short title
shortage
shortcoming
shorten
shortened
shortening
shorthand
shortly
shot
should
shoulder
shouldered
shouldering
shout
shove
shoved
shoving
show
showed
showing

shown
shrank
shrapnel
shred
shredded
shredding
shrewd
shrill
shrilly
shrine
shrink
shrinking
shroud
shrunk
shrunken
shun
shunned
shunning
shunt
shut
shutter
shutting
shuttle
shy
shyer
shyest
shying
shyly
shyness
si petitur tantum
sibilant
sic
sick
sick pay
sicken
sickened
sickening
sickly
side
sided
siding
siege

sift
sigh
sighed
sighing
sight
sighted
sighting
sign
signal
signalled
signalling
signatories
signatory
signature
signed
signet
significance
significant
signified
signify
signifying
signing
silence
silenced
silencer
silencing
silent
silicon
silicone
silk
sill
silo
silt
silver
similar
similarities
similarity
simile
similiter
simple
simplex commendatio
   non obligat

simpliciter
simplicity
simplification
simplified
simplify
simplifying
simply
simulate
simulated
simulating
simulation
simultaneous
sin
since
sincere
sincerely
sincerity
sine die
sine qua non
sinecure
sinful
sinfully
single
single bills
singled
singling
singly
singular
singular successor
singularity
singuli in solidum
sinister
sink
sinking
sinking-fund
sinned
sinning
sinus
sinuses
siphon
siphoned
siphoning

sir
sire
siren
sist
sister
sister-in-law
sisterly
sistor
sit
site
sited
sit-in
siting
sitting
situated
situation
six
sixteen
sixteenth
sixth
sixtieth
sixty
sizable
size
sizeable
sized
sizing
skein
skeletal
skeleton
sketch
sketches
sketchily
sketchy
skid
skidded
skidding
skies
skilful
skilfully
skill
skilled

skim
skimmed
skimming
skimp
skimpily
skimpy
skin
skinned
skinning
skipper
skirmish
skirmishes
skirting
skulk
skull
sky
slack
slacken
slackened
slackening
slag
slake
slaked
slaking
slam
slammed
slamming
slander
slander of goods
slander of title
slandered
slandering
slanderous
slang
slant
slap
slapped
slapping
slash
slashes
slat
slate

slated
slating
slatted
slaughter
slaughtered
slaughtering
slave
slavery
slavish
sleep
sleeper
sleepily
sleeping
sleeping partner
sleepy
sleeve
sleight-of-hand
slept
sleuth
slew
slewed
slewing
slice
sliced
slicing
slick
slid
slide
sliding
slight
slightly
slightness
slim
slimmed
slimming
sling
slinging
slink
slinkily
slinking
slinky
slip

slipped
slippery
slipping
slit
slitting
slogan
slope
sloped
sloping
sloppily
sloppy
slot
slothful
slothfully
slotted
slotting
slouch
slough
sloughed
sloughing
slovenly
slow
sluggish
sluice
slum
slumber
slumbered
slumbering
slump
slung
slunk
slur
slurred
slurring
slut
sluttish
sly
slyly
slyness
small
small claim
smallness

smart
smash
smashes
smattering
smear
smeared
smearing
smell
smelled
smelling
smelly
smelt
smelted
smelting
smile
smiled
smiling
smirk
smithereens
smithy
smitten
smog
smoke
smoked
smokeless
smoker
smoking
smoky
smooth
smoothed
smoothing
smother
smothered
smothering
smoulder
smouldered
smouldering
smudge
smudged
smudging
smug
smuggle

smuggled
smuggler
smuggling
smut
smutty
snag
snagged
snagging
snap
snapped
snappily
snapping
snappy
snare
snared
snaring
snatch
snatches
sneak
sneaky
sneer
sneered
sneering
sniff
snigger
sniggered
sniggering
snip
snipe
sniped
sniper
sniping
snipped
snipping
snivel
snivelled
snivelling
snob
snobbery
snobbish
snoop
snooped

snooping
snore
snored
snoring
snout
snow
snowed
snowing
snowy
snub
snubbed
snubbing
snuff
snug
so
soak
soar
soared
soaring
sob
sobbed
sobbing
sober
sobered
sobering
soberness
sobriety
socage
soccer
sociability
sociable
sociableness
sociably
social
social security
Social Security
   Tribunal
socialism
socialist
socialistic
socially
Society of Advocates

Ss

socioeconomic
sociological
sociology
socius criminis
socket
sodden
sodomy
soft
soften
softened
softening
software
soil
soiled
soiling
sojourn
sojourned
sojourning
solace
solaced
solacing
solar
solatium
sold
solder
soldered
soldering
soldier
soldiered
soldiering
sole
solely
solemn
solemn form
solemn procedure
solemnity
solemnly
solicit
solicited
soliciting
solicitor
Solicitor-General

Solicitors before the
    Supreme Court
    (SSC)
Solicitors Disciplinary
    Tribunal
solicitous
solid
solidarity
solidary
solidified
solidify
solidifying
solidity
soliloquies
soliloquy
solitary
solitude
solo
soloist
solubility
soluble
solum
solus
solution
solve
solved
solvency
solvent
solvent abuse
solving
solvitur ambulando
sombre
sombrely
sombreness
some
somebody
someone
somersault
something
somnambulant
somnambulism
somnolence

somnolent
son
sonic
son-in-law
sonorous
soon
sooner
soothe
soothed
soothing
sophisticated
sophistication
soporific
sordid
sore
sorely
soreness
sorrow
sorrowful
sorrowfully
sorry
sort
sortie
SOS
sotto voce
sought
soul
soulful
soulfully
sound
sour
source
southerly
southern
sovereign
sovereignty
sovereignty of
    Parliament
sow
sowed
sower
sowing

sown
space
spacecraft
spaced
spacing
spacious
spaciousness
span
Spanish
spank
spanking
spanned
spanner
spanning
spar
spare
spared
sparing
sparingly
spark
sparred
sparring
sparse
sparsely
spartan
spasm
spasmodic
spasmodically
spastic
spat
spate
spatial
spatter
spattered
spattering
spatula
spawn
speak
speaking
spear
special
special agent

special business
special case
special damages
special defence
special destination
special endorsement
special plea
special resolution
special service
special verdict
specialist
specialities
speciality
specialization
specialize
specialized
specializing
specially
specialties
specialty
species
specific
specific implement
specific intent
specific performance
specifically
specificatio
specification
specified
specify
specifying
specimen
specious
spectacle
spectacles
spectacular
spectacularly
spectator
spectra
spectrum
spectrums
speculate

speculated
speculating
speculation
speculative
speculatively
sped
speech
speeches
speechless
speed
speeded
speedily
speeding
speedometer
speedy
spei emptio
spell
spelled
spelling
spelt
spend
spending
spent
spent conviction
sperm
spes successionis
sphere
spherical
spied
spiel
spies
spike
spiked
spiky
spill
spillage
spilled
spilling
spilt
spin
spinal
spindly

spine
spineless
spinney
spinning
spin-off
spinster
spiral
spiralled
spiralling
spire
spirit
spirited
spiriting
spiritual
spiritualism
spiritualist
spiritually
spit
spite
spiteful
spitefully
spitting
spittle
spittoon
splash
splashes
spleen
splice
spliced
splicing
splint
splinter
splintered
splintering
split
splitting
spoil
spoiled
spoiling
spoilt
spoke
spoken

spokesman
sponge
sponged
sponging
sponsio ludicra
sponsored
sponsoring
spontaneity
spontaneous
spool
spoon
spooned
spooning
sporadic
sporadically
sport
sporting
sportsman
sportsmanlike
sportsmen
spot
spotless
spotlight
spotted
spotting
spouse
spout
spouted
spouting
sprain
sprained
spraining
sprang
sprawl
spray
sprayed
spraying
spread
spread-eagled
spreading
spree
spring

springing
springing use
sprinkle
sprinkled
sprinkler
sprinkling
sprint
sprinter
sprout
sprouted
sprouting
spruce
sprucely
sprung
spry
spryly
spuilzie
spun
spur
spurious
spurn
spurred
spurring
spurt
sputum
spy
spying
squabble
squabbled
squabbling
squad
squadron
squalid
squall
squally
squalor
squander
squandered
squandering
square
squarely
squash

squat
squatted
squatter
squatting
squeamish
squeeze
squeezed
squeezing
squint
squire
stab
stabbed
stabbing
stability
stabilize
stabilized
stabilizer
stabilizing
stable
stack
staff
staffed
staffing
stag
stage
staged
stagflation
stagger
staggered
staggering
staging
stagnant
stagnate
stagnated
stagnating
stagnation
staid
stain
stained
staining
stainless
stair

stake
staked
stakeholder
staking
stale
stale cheque
stalemate
stall
stalwart
stamina
stamp
stamp duty
stance
stanch
stand
standard
standard charge
standard form
standard security
standardization
standardize
standardized
standardizing
standby
stand-in
standing
standing committee
standstill
staple
starboard
stare decisis
start
startle
startled
startling
starvation
starve
starved
starving
state
state of emergency
stated

stated case
stateless
stately
statement
statesman
statesmanlike
statesmen
static
stating
station
stationary
stationer
stationery
statistical
statistically
statistician
statistics
stature
status
status quo
status quo ante
statute
statute-barred
statutory
statutory duty
statutory instrument
   (SI)
statutory rules and
   orders (SR & O)
statutory small
   tenancy
statutory tenancy
staunch
stave
staved
staving
stay
stay of execution
stayed
staying
steadfast
steadied

steadily
steadiness
steady
steadying
steal
stealing
stealth
stealthily
stealthy
steel
steep
steer
steered
steering
stem
stemmed
stemming
stench
stentorian
step
stepmother
stepped
stepping
stereo
stereophonic
stereotype
stereotyped
sterile
sterility
sterilization
sterilize
sterilized
sterilizing
sterling
stern
sternness
stertorous
stet
stethoscope
stevedore
steward
stewardess

stewardesses
stick
stickiness
sticking
stickler
sticky
stiff
stiffen
stiffened
stiffening
stifle
stifled
stifling
stigma
stiletto
still
stillborn
stillness
stilted
stimulant
stimulate
stimulated
stimulating
stimuli
stimulus
sting
stinging
stint
stipend
stipendiary magistrate
stipulate
stipulated
stipulating
stipulation
stir
stirred
stirring
stock
stock exchange
stockade
stockbroker
stocked

stocking
stock-jobber
stocktaking
stoic
stoical
stoically
stoicism
stole
stolen
stolid
stolidity
stomach
stone
stood
stop
stop and search
stoppage
stoppage in transitu
stopped
stopping
storage
store
stored
storey
storing
storm
stove
stow
stowaway
straddle
straddled
straddling
straight
straighten
straightened
straightening
straightness
strain
strained
straining
strait
straitened

straitjacket
straitlaced
strand
strange
strangely
strangeness
stranger
strangers in blood
strangle
strangled
stranglehold
strangling
strangulation
strap
strapped
strapping
strata
stratagem
strategic
strategically
strategies
strategist
strategy
stratification
stratified
stratum
stray
strayed
straying
streak
stream
streamed
streaming
streamline
streamlined
streamlining
street
street trading
strength
strengthen
strengthened
strengthening

strenuous
stress
stressed
stresses
stressing
stretch
stretcher
stretches
strew
strewed
strewing
strewn
stricken
strict
strict liability
stricti juris
stricture
stride
stridency
strident
striding
strife
strike
striking
striking off
string
stringencies
stringency
stringent
stringing
strip
stripped
stripping
strive
striven
striving
strode
stroke
stroked
stroking
strong
strove

struck
structural
structurally
structure
structured
struggle
struggled
struggling
strung
strychnine
stubble
stubborn
stubbornness
stucco
stuck
student
studied
studies
studio
studious
studiousness
study
studying
stultified
stultify
stultifying
stump
stun
stung
stunned
stunning
stupefaction
stupefied
stupefy
stupefying
stupendous
stupid
stupidity
stupor
sturdily
sturdiness
sturdy

Ss

stutter
stuttered
stuttering
style
styled
styling
stylus
styluses
suave
suavely
suavity
sub judice
sub modo
sub nom
sub nomine
sub rosa
sub silentio
sub tit
sub titulo
sub voce
subaltern
subcommittee
subconscious
subdue
subdued
subduing
subinfeudation
subject
subject to contract
subjective
subjectively
subjectiveness
subjectivity
subjugate
subjugated
subjugating
subjugation
sub-lease
sub-letting
sublieutenant
sublime
sublimely

sublimity
submarine
submerge
submerged
submerging
submersion
submission
submissive
submissively
submit
submitted
submitting
subordinate
subordinate legislation
subordinated
subordinating
suborn
subornation
subornation of perjury
suborned
suborning
subpoena
subpoenaed
subpoenaing
subrogate
subrogation
subscribe
subscribed
subscribing
subscription
subsequent
subservience
subservient
subside
subsided
subsidence
subsidiaries
subsidiary
subsidiary company
subsidies
subsiding
subsidize

subsidized
subsidizing
subsidy
subsist
subsistence
subsoil
substance
substantial
substantially
substantiate
substantiated
substantiating
substantive
substitute
substituted
substituting
substitution
substitutional
substitutional legacy
substitutionary
substratum
sub-tenancy
sub-tenant
subterfuge
subterranean
subtitle
subtle
subtleties
subtlety
subtly
subtract
subtraction
sub-trust
suburb
suburban
suburbia
subversive
subversively
subway
succeed
succeeded
succeeding

success
successes
successful
successfully
succession
successive
successively
successor
succinct
succinctly
succour
succoured
succouring
succumb
succumbed
succumbing
such
suction
sudden
suddenly
suddenness
sue
sued
suffer
sufferance
suffered
suffering
suffice
sufficed
sufficient
sufficing
suffix
suffixes
suffocate
suffocated
suffocating
suffocation
suffrage
suffragette
suffuse
suffused
suffusing

suffusion
suggest
suggestible
suggestio falsi
suggestion
suggestive
suggestively
sui generis
sui juris
suicidal
suicide
suicide pact
suing
suit
suitability
suitable
suitably
suitcase
suite
suited
suiting
suitor
sullied
sully
sullying
sulphur
sulphuric
sum
summar roll
summaries
summarily
summarize
summarized
summarizing
summary
summary application
summary cause
summary conviction
summary diligence
summary dismissal
summary jurisdiction
summary warrant

summed
summing
summing-up
summit
summon
summoned
summoning
summons
summons for
   directions
summonses
sumptuous
Sunday
sunk
sunken
superannuated
superannuation
supercargo
supercilious
superficial
superficially
superficies solo cedit
superfluity
superfluous
superintend
superintendence
superintendent
superior
superior courts
superiority
superlative
superlatively
supermarket
supernatural
supernaturally
supersede
supersedeas
superseded
superseding
supersonic
superstition
superstitious

superstitiously
supervening
supervening cause
supervening event
supervise
supervised
supervising
supervision
supervisor
supine
supplant
supple
supplement
supplementary
suppleness
suppliant
supplication
supplied
supplies
supply
supplying
support
supporter
suppose
supposed
supposedly
supposing
supposition
suppress
suppressio veri,
   suggestio falsi
suppression
suppurate
suppurated
suppurating
supra protest
supremacy
supreme
Supreme Court
supremely
surcharge
sure

surely
sureties
surety
surface
surfaced
surfacing
surfeit
surge
surged
surgeon
surgeries
surgery
surgical
surgically
surging
surlily
surliness
surly
surmise
surmised
surmising
surmountable
surname
surpass
surplice
surplus
surplusage
surprise
surprised
surprising
surrebutter
surrejoinder
surrender
surrender value
surrendered
surrendering
surreptitious
surrogate
surrogate mother
surrogatum
surround
surroundings

surtax
surveillance
survey
surveyed
surveying
surveyor
survival
survive
survived
surviving
survivor
survivorship
susceptibility
susceptible
suspect
suspend
suspended
suspended sentence
suspense
suspension
suspension and
   interdict
suspension and
   liberation
suspensive condition
suspicion
suspicious
sustain
sustained
sustaining
sustenance
swab
swabbed
swabbing
swagger
swaggered
swaggering
swallow
swap
swapped
swapping
swarm

swarthy
swathed
sway
swayed
swaying
swear
swearing
sweat
sweated
sweating
Swedish
sweep
sweeping
sweepstake
swell
swelled
swelling
swept
swerve
swerved
swerving
swift
swiftness
swig
swigged
swigging
swill
swindle
swindled
swindler
swindling
swing
swingeing
swinging
swipe
swiped
swiping
Swiss
switch
switchboard
switches
swivel

swivelled
swivelling
swollen
swop
swopped
swopping
swore
sworn
swung
sycophant
syllabi
syllabic
syllable
syllabus
syllabuses
symbol
symbolic
symbolically
symbolism
symbolize
symbolized
symbolizing
symmetrical
symmetrically
symmetry
sympathetic
sympathetically
sympathize
sympathized
sympathizing
sympathy
symposium
symptom
symptomatic
synagogue
synallagmatic
synchronize
synchronized
synchronizing
syndicate
synod
synonym

synonymous
synopses
synopsis
syntax
synthesis
synthesize
synthesized
synthesizing
synthetic
synthetically
syringe
system
systematic
systematically

Tt

table
tableau
tableaux
tabled
tablet
tabling
tabloid
tabulate
tabulated
tabulating
tacit
tacit relocation
taciturn
taciturnity
tack
tack duty
tacking
tackle
tackled
tackling
tacky

Tt

tact	tamed	tarnish
tactful	tamely	tarpaulin
tactfully	taming	tarred
tactical	tamper	tarried
tactically	tampered	tarring
tactician	tampering	tarry
tactics	tangent	tarrying
tactless	tangible	tartar
tag	tangible property	task
tagged	tangibly	taste
tagging	tangle	tasted
tail	tangled	tasteful
tail general	tangling	tastefully
tail male general	tank	tasteless
tail male special	tankard	tasting
tailed	tanker	tattered
tailing	tanneries	tatters
tailor	tannery	tattoo
tailored	tannin	tattooed
tailoring	tantalize	tattooing
tailzie	tantalized	taught
taint	tantalizing	taunt
take	tantamount to	taut
take silk	tap	tauten
take-home pay	tape	tautened
taken	tape recorder	tautening
takeover	taped	tautological
taking	taper	tautologically
taking silk	tape-recording	tautology
tale	tapered	tavern
talent	tapering	tawdry
talented	taping	tax
talisman	tapped	tax avoidance
talk	tapping	tax evasion
talkative	tar	tax haven
tall	tardily	tax year
tallied	tardy	taxable
tallies	tare	taxation
tallness	target	taxation of costs
tally	tariff	taxi
tallying	tarmac	taxidermist
tame	tarmacadam	taxidermy

taxied
taxiing
taxing
teach
teacher
teaching
team
teamed
teaming
tear
tearing
technical
technicalities
technicality
technically
technician
technique
technological
technologically
technologies
technologist
technology
tedious
tedium
teem
teemed
teeming
teenage
teenager
teens
teeth
teetotal
teetotaller
teind
Teind Court
teind roll
telecommunication
telegram
telegraph
telegraphic
telepathic
telepathically

telepathy
telephone
telephoned
telephoning
telephonist
telephoto lens
telescope
telescoped
telescopic
telescopically
telescoping
teletext
televise
televised
televising
television
telex
tell
teller
telling
temerity
temper
temperament
temperamental
temperamentally
temperance
temperate
temperature
tempered
tempering
temporal
temporal peer
temporary
temporary sheriff
temporize
temporized
temporizing
tempt
temptation
tempting
ten
tenable

tenacious
tenacity
tenancies
tenancy
tenancy at sufferance
tenancy at will
tenancy by estoppel
tenant
tenant by the curtesy
tenant for life
tenant in tail
tenantable repair
tenanted
tend
tendencies
tendency
tendendas
tender
tender of amends
tendered
tendering
tendon
tenement
tenendas
tenet
tenor
tense
tensely
tension
tentative
tentatively
tenth
tenuous
tenure
terce
tercentenary
term
term of years
Termes de la Ley
terminal
terminate
terminated

terminating
termination
termini
terminology
terminus
terminuses
termly
termor
terra firma
terrace
terracing
terrain
terrestrial
terrible
terribly
terrified
terrify
terrifying
territorial
territorial waters
territoriality
territories
territory
terror
terrorism
terrorist
terrorize
terrorized
terrorizing
terse
tersely
terseness
tertiary
tertium quid
tertius
test
test case
testable
testacy
testament
testamentary
testamentary capacity

testamentary intention
testamentary trust
testamentary writing
testate
testator
testatrix
testatum
teste
testicle
testified
testify
testifying
testimonial
testimonial evidence
testimonies
testimonium
testimony
testing clause
tetanus
tether
tethered
tethering
text
textbook
textile
textual
texture
than
thank
thankful
thankfully
thankless
thanksgiving
that
thatch
thatched
thatching
thaw
the
theatre
theatrical
theatrically

thee
theft
their
theirs
them
theme
themselves
then
thence
theodolite
theologian
theological
theology
theorem
theoretic
theoretical
theoretically
theories
theorize
theorized
theorizing
theory
therapeutic
therapist
therapy
there
thereabouts
therefore
therm
thermal
thermostat
thesaurus
these
these presents
theses
thesis
they
they'd
they'll
they're
thick
thicken

thickened
thickening
thicket
thickness
thicknesses
thief
thieves
thievish
thigh
thin
thing
thing in action
think
thinking
thinned
thinner
thinness
thinnest
thinning
third
third party
third-rate
thirlage
thirst
thirstily
thirsty
thirteen
thirteenth
thirtieth
thirty
this
thole
thole an assize
tholing an assize
thong
thorax
thorn
thorny
thorough
thoroughfare
thoroughgoing
those

thou
though
thought
thoughtful
thoughtfully
thoughtfulness
thoughtless
thousand
thousandth
thrall
thrash
thread
threat
threaten
threatened
threatening
three
thresh
threshold
threw
thrice
thrift
thriftily
thrifty
thrill
thriller
thrilling
thrive
thrived
thriving
throat
throb
throbbed
throbbing
throes
thromboses
thrombosis
throne
throng
throttle
throttled
throttling

through
throughout
throughput
throw
throwing
thrown
thrust
thrusting
thug
thumb
Thursday
thus
thwart
thwarted
thwarting
thyroid
tiara
ticket
tidal
tide
tidied
tidier
tidiest
tidily
tidiness
tidings
tidy
tidying
tie
tied
tied cottage
tied house
tier
tight
tighten
tightened
tightening
tightness
till
tilled
tiller
tilling

tilt
timber
timbre
time
time charter
time immemorial
time out of mind
time-bar
timed
timely
timeous
timetable
timid
timidity
timing
timorous
tin
tin parachute
tinder
tinge
tinged
tinging
tinker
tinkered
tinkering
tinned
tinning
tiny
tip
tipped
tipping
tirade
tire
tired
tireless
tiresome
tiring
tissue
tithe
titivate
titivated
titivating

title
title deeds
title to exclude
title to sue
titled
titular
to
toadied
toady
toadying
tobacco
today
toe
together
toil
toiled
toilet
toiling
token
told
tolerable
tolerably
tolerance
tolerate
tolerated
tolerating
toleration
toll
tomb
tombstone
tome
Tomlin Order
tomorrow
ton
tone
toned
tongue
tonic
tonight
toning
tonnage
tonne

tonsilitis
tonsils
tonsure
tontine
too
took
tool
tooling
tooth
top
topaz
toper
topic
topical
topically
topmost
topography
topping
topple
toppled
toppling
torch
torches
tore
Tories
torment
tormentor
torn
torpedo
torpedoed
torpedoes
torpedoing
torpid
torpor
torrent
torrential
torrid
torso
tort
tort of conspiracy
tort of conversion
tortfeasor

tortious
tortuous
torture
tortured
torturing
Tory
toss
tot
tot up
total
total loss
totalitarian
totalled
totalling
totally
tote
toties quoties
totted up
totter
tottered
tottering
totting up
touch
touchily
touchiness
touching
touchy
tough
toughen
toughened
toughening
toupee
tour
toured
touring
tourism
tourist
tourniquet
tout
touted
touting
tow

toward
towards
towed
tower
towered
towering
towing
town
toxic
toxin
trace
traceable
traced
tracery
tracing
track
tract
traction
tractor
trade
trade description
trade mark
trade secret
trade union
trade unionist
traded
trade-in
trademark
tradename
trader
tradesman
trading
tradition
traditional
traditionally
traffic
traffic warden
trafficked
trafficking
tragedies
tragedy
tragic

tragically
trail
trailed
trailer
trailing
train
trained
trainee
trainer
training
trait
traitor
traitorous
tram
trammel
trammelled
trammelling
tramp
trample
trampled
trampling
tranquillizer
transaction
transatlantic
transceiver
transcend
transcended
transcending
transept
transfer
transferable
transferee
transference
transferor
transferred
transferring
transfiguration
transfix
transform
transformation

transfuse
transfusion
transgression
transience
transient
transistor
transit
transition
transitional
transitive
transitorily
transitory
translate
translated
translating
translation
translator
translucence
translucent
transmission
transmit
transmitted
transmitter
transmitting
transparencies
transparency
transparent
transpire
transpired
transpiring
transplant
transport
transportation
transpose
transposed
transposing
transposition
transverse
trap
trapped
trapper
trapping

trauma
traumatic
travaux préparatoires
travel
travelled
traveller
traveller's cheque
travelling
traverse
traversed
traversing
travesty
trawl
trawled
trawler
trawling
treacherous
treachery
tread
treason
treason felony
treasonable
treasure
treasurer
treasure-trove
treasuries
treasury
Treasury Counsel
Treasury Solicitor
treat
treaties
treating
treatise
treatment
treaty
trek
trekked
trekking
tremendous
tremor
tremulous
trench

trenchant
trenches
trend
trepidation
trespass
trespass by relation
trespasser
trespasses
trespassing
trespassory
trestle
trial
triangle
triangular
tribal
tribe
tribulation
tribunal
tribune
tributaries
tributary
tribute
trice
trick
trickery
trickle
trickled
trickling
trickster
tricky
tricolour
tried
triennial
tries
trifle
trifled
trifling
trigger
trigger clause
triggered
triggering
trigonometry

trilogies
trilogy
trim
trimmed
trimming
Trinity
trinket
trio
trip
triple
triplet
triplicate
tripod
tripped
tripping
trite
triumph
triumphal
triumphant
triumphed
triumphing
trivial
trivialities
triviality
trod
trodden
trolley
troop
trooped
trooper
trooping
trophies
trophy
trouble
troubled
troublesome
troubling
trough
troupe
trover
truancy
truant

truce
truck
truculent
trudge
trudged
trudging
true
truism
truly
trump
truncated
truncheon
trundle
trundled
trundling
trunk
truss
trussed
trusses
trussing
trust
trust deed
trust deed for creditors
trust instrument
trust territory
trustee
trustee de son tort
trustee in bankruptcy
trustee in
    sequestration
trusteeship
trustful
trustfully
trusting
trustworthy
trusty
truth
truthful
truthfully
truthfulness
try
trying

tube
tuberculosis
tubing
tubular
tuck
Tuesday
tuft
tug
tugged
tugging
tug-of-war
tuition
tumble
tumbled
tumbling
tumour
tumult
tumultuous
tun
tunnel
tunnelled
tunnelling
turban
turbary
turbine
turbulence
turbulent
turf
turgid
Turkish
turmoil
turn
turning
turning Queen's
    evidence
turnover
turnstile
turntable
turpentine
turpis causa
turret
turreted

Uu

tussle
tutor
tutor dative
tutor nominate
tutor-at-law
tutorial
tutrix
tweezers
twelfth
twelve
twentieth
twenty
twice
twig
twilight
twin
twine
twined
twinge
twining
twist
two
twofold
tycoon
tying
type
typed
typewriter
typhoid
typhoon
typhus
typical
typically
typified
typify
typifying
typing
typist
tyrannical
tyrannically
tyrannize
tyrannized

tyrannizing
tyrannous
tyranny
tyrant
tyre

Uu

uberrimae fidei
ubi jus ibi remedium
ubiquitous
udal land
udal tenure
uglier
ugliest
ugliness
ugly
ulcer
ulterior
ulterior intent
ultimata
ultimate
ultimately
ultimatum
ultimatums
ultimus haeres
ultra vires
ultrasonic
ultraviolet
umbilical
umbrage
umpire
umpired
umpiring
umquhile
unable
unaccountable

unaccountably
unadulterated
unanimity
unanimous
unapproachable
unascertained
unassuming
unaware
unawares
unbalanced
unbend
unbending
unbent
unborn
unbridled
unburden
unburdened
unburdening
uncalled capital
uncalled for
uncannily
uncanniness
uncanny
uncared for
uncertain
uncharted
uncle
uncoil
uncoiled
uncoiling
uncollected
uncommon
uncompromising
unconscionable
unconscionable
   bargain
unconscious
unconscious bailee
unconsciously
uncouth
undaunted
undefended cause

undeniable
undeniably
under
undercapitalized
undercarriage
underclothes
undercover
undercurrent
undercut
undercutting
underdeveloped
underdog
underdone
underestimate
underestimated
underestimating
underfoot
undergo
undergoing
undergone
undergraduate
underground
undergrowth
underhand
underline
underlined
underlining
underlying
undermine
undermined
undermining
underneath
underprivileged
underrate
underrated
underrating
undersigned
underskirt
understand
understandable
understandably
understanding

understate
understated
understatement
understating
understood
understudied
understudy
understudying
undertake
undertaken
undertaker
undertaking
undertone
undertook
undervalue
undervalued
undervaluing
underwear
underwent
underworld
underwrite
underwriter
underwriting
underwritten
underwrote
undid
undischarged
undisclosed principal
undivided
undo
undoing
undone
undoubted
undress
undue
undue influence
undulate
undulated
undulating
unduly
unearned
unearth

unearthly
uneasily
uneasy
unemployed
unemployment
unenforceable
unequal
unequalled
unequivocal
unequivocally
unerring
uneven
unexpected
unexpected balance
   of established
   development value
   (uxb)
unfailing
unfair
unfair contract terms
unfair dismissal
unfaithful
unfasten
unfastened
unfastening
unfavourable
unfit
unfit to plead
unfitness
unfitted
unflagging
unflinching
unfold
unforgettable
unforgettably
unfortunate
unfortunately
unfounded
unfurl
ungainly
ungracious
ungrateful

ungratefully
unguarded
unhappily
unhappiness
unhappy
unhealthily
unhealthy
unhinge
unhinged
unhinging
unicorn
unification
unified
uniform
uniformity
unify
unifying
unilateral
unincorporated
unintentional
uninterrupted
union
unique
uniquely
unison
unit
unitary
unite
united
United Kingdom
United Nations
uniting
unity
unity of seisin
universal
universal agent
universal successor
universally
universe
universities
university
unjust enrichment

unkempt
unkind
unlawful
unlawfully
unleash
unless
unlikely
unlimited company
unliquidated
unload
unloaded
unloading
unlooked for
unloose
unloosed
unloosing
unluckily
unlucky
unmanly
unmask
unmentionable
unmistakable
unmistakably
unmitigated
unmoved
unnatural
unnecessarily
unnecessary
unobtrusive
unobtrusively
unopposed
unpack
unpaid
unpaid seller's lien
unpalatable
unparalleled
unpick
unpremeditated
unprepossessing
unpretentious
unprincipled
unravel

unravelled
unravelling
unread
unreasonable
unregistered
unremitting
unreported
unrequited
unrest
unrivalled
unruliness
unruly
unsavoury
unscathed
unscrew
unseasonable
unsecured
unseen
unsettled
unsightly
unsolicited
unsophisticated
unsound
unsound mind
unspeakable
unspeakably
unstructured
unstudied
unsuspecting
unsworn
unthinkable
until
untimely
unto
untold
untoward
untrue
untruth
untruthful
untruthfully
unusual
unusually

unvarnished
unveil
unveiled
unveiling
unwanted
unwieldy
unwitting
unwonted
unworthy
up
upbraid
upbraided
upbraiding
upbringing
upgrade
upgraded
upgrading
upheaval
upheld
uphill
uphold
upholder
upholding
upholster
upholstered
upholsterer
upholstering
upholstery
upkeep
upland
uplift
upmost
upon
upper
uppermost
upright
uprising
uproar
uproarious
uproot
uprooted
uprooting

upset
upset price
upsetting
upshot
upside-down
upstairs
upstanding
upstart
upstream
uptake
up-to-date
uranium
urban
urbane
urbanities
urchin
urge
urged
urgency
urgent
urging
urinary
urinate
urinated
urinating
urine
urine test
urn
us
usage
use
used
useful
usefully
usefulness
useless
user
usher
ushered
usherette
ushering
using

usque ad medium
  filum aquae (or
  viae)
usual
usual covenant
usually
usucapion
usufruct
usufructuary
usurp
usurpation
usury
ut intus
ut supra
utensil
uteri
uterine
uterus
utilities
utility
utilization
utilize
utilized
utilizing
utmost
utter
utter Bar
utterance
uttered
uttering
utterly

Vv

vacancies
vacancy
vacant
vacant possession

vacate
vacated
vacating
vacation
vacation sitting
vaccinate
vaccinated
vaccinating
vaccine
vacillate
vacillated
vacillating
vacuous
vacuum
vagabond
vagaries
vagary
vagina
vagrancy
vagrant
vague
vaguely
vagueness
vain
vale
valencies
valency
valet
valiant
valid
validate
validity
valley
valorous
valour
valuable
valuation
valuator
value
value received
value-added tax (VAT)
valued

valuer
valuing
valve
van
vandal
vandalism
vandalize
vandalized
vandalizing
vane
vanguard
vanish
vanities
vanity
vanquish
vantage
vapid
vaporize
vaporizer
vaporizing
vapour
variable
variably
variance
variant
variation
varicose
varied
variegated
varieties
variety
various
varnish
varnishes
vary
varying
vassal
vast
vat
vault
vaunt
veal

veer
veered
veering
vegetarian
vegetate
vegetated
vegetating
vegetation
vehemence
vehement
vehicle
vehicular
veil
veiled
veiling
vein
veined
vellum
velocities
velocity
venal
vendee
vendetta
vending
vendor
veneer
venerable
venerate
venerated
venerating
veneration
venereal disease (VD)
vengeance
vengeful
venia aetatis
venial
venire de novo
venire facias
venison
venom
venomous
vent

ventilate
ventilated
ventilating
ventilation
ventilator
ventricle
ventriloquism
ventriloquist
venture
ventured
venturing
venue
veracity
veranda
verandah
verb
verba chartarum
  fortius accipiuntur
  contra proferentem
verba ita sunt
  intelligenda ut res
  magis valeat quam
  pereat
verbal
verbal injury
verbally
verbatim
verbose
verbosity
verdant
verdict
verdigris
verdure
verge
verged
vergens ad inopiam
verger
verging
verification
verified
verify
verifying

verily
veritable
veritably
veritas
veritas convicii
vermin
verminous
vernacular
vernal
versatile
versatility
verse
version
versus (v)
vertebra
vertebrae
vertebrate
vertex
vertical
vertically
vertices
vertigo
verve
very
vespers
vessel
vest
vested
vested in interest
vested in possession
vestibule
vestige
vestigial
vesting
vesting subject to
  defeasance
vestries
vestry
vet
veteran
veterinary surgeon
veto

vetoed
vetoes
vetoing
vetted
vetting
vex
vexation
vexatious
vexatious action
vexatious litigant
vexed
vexing
vi et armis
via
viable
viaduct
vibrate
vibrated
vibrating
vibration
vicar
vicarious
vicarious liability
vicarious responsibility
vice
vice versa
Vice-Chancellor (V-C)
viceroy
vicinity
vicious
vicissitude
victim
victimization
victimize
victimized
victimizing
victor
victories
victorious
victory
victuals
vide

Vv

videlicet
video
videotape
vidimus
viduity
vie
vied
view
viewdata
viewpoint
vigil
vigilance
vigilant
vigilante
vigorous
vigour
vile
vilified
vilify
vilifying
villa
village
villager
villain
villainies
villainous
villainy
vindicate
vindicated
vindicating
vindictive
vindictively
vine
vinegar
vineyard
vintage
violate
violated
violating
violation
violence
violent

violent disorder
violent profits
virgin
virginal
virginity
virile
virility
virtual
virtually
virtue
virtuosity
virtuoso
virtuous
virtute officii
virulence
virulent
virus
viruses
vis et metus
vis major
visa
visage
vis-à-vis
viscera
viscid
viscosity
viscount
viscountess
viscountesses
viscous
visibility
visible
visibly
vision
visionaries
visionary
visit
visitation
visited
visiting
visitor
visor

vista
visual
visualize
visualized
visualizing
visually
vital
vitality
vitally
vitamins
vitious intromission
vitium reale
vitreous
vitrified
vitriol
vituperation
vituperative
viva voce
vivacious
vivacity
vivid
vividness
vivisection
viz
vocabularies
vocabulary
vocal
vocally
vocation
vocational
vociferous
vogue
voice
voiced
voicing
void
void for uncertainty
voidable
voir dire
volatile
volenti non fit injuria
volition

volley
volt
voltage
volte-face
volubility
voluble
volubly
volume
voluminous
voluntarily
voluntary
voluntary liquidation
voluntary waste
voluntary winding-up
volunteer
volunteered
volunteering
voluptuous
vomit
vomited
vomiting
voracious
voracity
vortex
vortexes
vortices
vote
voted
voting
voting shares
vouch
vouchee
voucher
vow
vowed
vowel
vowing
voyage
voyaged
voyaging
vulgar
vulgarity

vulnerable
vulture
vying

Ww

wad
wadding
waddle
waddled
waddling
wade
waded
wader
wading
wage
waged
wager
wagering
wages
waggon
waging
waif
wail
wailed
wailing
waist
wait
waiter
waiting-room
waitress
waive
waived
waiver
waiving
wake
waked
wakeful

waken
wakened
wakening
waking
walk
walkie-talkie
wall
wallet
wan
wander
wandered
wanderer
wandering
wanderlust
wane
waned
waning
want
wanton
war
ward
ward of court
warded
warden
warder
warding
wardrobe
wardship
ware
warehouse
warfare
warily
wariness
warlike
warm
warmth
warn
warning
warp
warpath
warrandice
warrant

Ww

warrant sale	wavered	weathervane
warrantor	wavering	weave
warranty	waving	weaver
warred	wax	weaving
warren	way	web
warring	way-bill	webbed
warrior	wayfarer	webbing
warship	waylaid	wed
wart	waylay	we'd
wary	waylaying	wedded
was	wayleave	wedding
wash	wayside	wedge
washer	wayward	wedged
wastage	we	wedging
waste	weak	wedlock
wasted	weaken	Wednesday
wasteful	weakened	week
wastefully	weakening	weekday
waster	weakling	weekend
wasting	weakly	weekly
wasting assets	weakness	weep
wastrel	wealth	weeping
watch	wealthier	weigh
watches	wealthiest	weighed
watchful	wealthy	weighing
watchfully	wean	weight
watchman	weaned	weights and measures
watchmen	weaning	weighty
water	weapon	weir
watered	wear	weird
waterfall	wear and tear	welcome
watering	wearable	welcomed
waterlogged	wearer	welcoming
waterproof	wearied	weld
watery	wearily	welder
watt	wearing	welfare
wattage	wearisome	well
wattle	weary	we'll
wave	wearying	well up
waved	weather	welled up
wavelength	weathered	welling up
waver	weathering	welt

welter	wherever	whittle
wend	wherewithal	whittled
went	whet	whittling
wept	whether	who
were	whetted	whoever
we're	whetting	whole
weren't	which	whole blood
west	whichever	wholesale
westerly	while	wholesaler
western	whilst	wholesome
westward	whim	who'll
westwards	whimsies	wholly
wet	whimsy	whom
wetness	whine	whore
wetter	whined	whose
wettest	whining	why
wetting	whip	wick
we've	whipped	wicked
wharf	whipping	wickedness
wharfs	whisker	wicket
wharves	whiskies	wide
what	whisky	widely
whatever	whisper	widen
whatsoever	whispered	widened
wheat	whispering	widening
wheaten	whist	widespread
wheedle	whistle	widow
wheedled	whistled	widower
wheedling	whistling	width
wheel	Whit	wield
wheelbarrow	whit	wielded
wheelchair	white	wielding
wheeled	white knight	wife
wheeling	white-collar worker	wig
when	whiten	wild
whence	whitened	wilderness
whenever	whiteness	wildness
where	whitening	wile
whereabouts	whitewash	wilful
whereas	whither	wilful imposition
wherefore	Whitsun	wilful misconduct
whereupon	Whitsunday	wilful neglect

Ww

wilful refusal
wilfully
will
willed
willing
wilt
wily
win
wince
winced
winch
winches
wincing
wind
wind up
winded
windfall
winding
winding-up
windmill
window
windscreen
wine
wing
winged
winning
winsome
winter
wintered
wintering
wintry
wipe
wiped
wiper
wiping
wire
wired
wireless
wiring
wiry
wisdom
wise

wisely
wish
wishes
wishful
wit
witchcraft
with
with profits
withdraw
withdrawal
withdrawing
withdrawn
withdrew
wither
withered
withering
withheld
withhold
withholding
within
without
without issue
without prejudice
withstand
withstanding
withstood
witness
witnesses
witticism
wittily
wittingly
witty
wives
woe
woeful
woefully
woke
woken
woman
womanhood
womanly
womb

women
won
wonder
wondered
wonderful
wonderfully
wondering
wont
won't
woo
wood
wooded
wooden
woodland
woodwork
wooed
wooer
wooing
Woolsack
word
wording
wordy
wore
work
work in progress
work to rule
workable
worker
work-in
working day
workman
workmanship
workmen
world
worldly
worn
worried
worries
worry
worrying
worse
worsen

worsened
worsening
worship
worshipful
worshipfully
worshipped
worshipping
worst
worsted
worth
worthily
worthless
worthy
would
would-be
wound
wounding
wove
woven
wrangle
wrangled
wrangling
wrap
wrapped
wrapper
wrapping
wrath
wrathful
wrathfully
wreak
wreaked
wreaking
wreath
wreathe
wreathed
wreathing
wreck
wreckage
wrecked
wrecking
wrench
wrenches

wrest
wrestle
wrestled
wrestler
wrestling
wretched
wring
wringing
wrist
writ
write
writer
Writer to Her
    Majesty's Signet
    (WS)
writhe
writhed
writhing
writing
written
wrong
wrongdoer
wrongful
wrongfully
wrote
wrought-iron
wrung
wry

Xx

xenophobia
xenophobic
Xerox®
X-ray
X-rayed
X-raying
xylophone

Yy

yacht
yachting
yachtsman
yard
yardstick
yarn
year
year and day
year to year
yearly
yearn
yeast
yellow
yen
yeoman
yes
yesses
yesterday
yet
yew
yield
yoga
yoke
Yom Kippur
yonder
yore
York-Antwerp rules
you
you'd
you'll
young
young offender
youngster
your
you're
yourselves
youth
youth custody

youthful
youthfully
you've
Yugoslavian
Yule

Zz

zeal
zealot
zealous

zealous witness
zebra crossing
zenith
zephyr
zero
zero rating
zest
zestful
zestfully
zigzag
zigzagged
zigzagging
zinc

zip
zipped
zipping
zodiac
zone

Appendices

Words liable to be confused

aboard
abroad

accept
except

access
excess

addition
edition

adverse
averse

advice
advise

aesthetic
ascetic

affect
effect

affluent
effluent

air
heir

all
awl

allay
alley
ally

allegory
allergy

alley
allay
ally

alliterate
illiterate

allowed
aloud

allude
elude

allusion
delusion
illusion

aloud
allowed

ally
allay
alley

altar
alter

alteration
altercation

alternately
alternatively

amateur
amateurish

amend
emend

amiable
amicable

among
between

amoral
immoral
immortal

anecdote
antidote

angel
angle

annals
annuals

annex
annexe

annuals
annals

antidote
anecdote

antiquated
antique

appraise
apprise

arc
ark

arisen
arose

arose
arisen

artist
artiste

ascent
assent

ascetic
aesthetic

assay
essay

assent
ascent

ate
eaten

aural
oral

averse
adverse

awl
all

axes
axis

bad
bade

bade
bid

bail
bale
bale out

baited
bated

bale
bale out
bail

ballet
ballot

banns
bans

bare
bear

barn
baron
barren

base
bass

bated
baited

baton
batten

bazaar
bizarre

be
bee

bean
been
being

bear
bare

beat
beaten

beat
beet

beau
bow

became
become

bee
be

been
bean
being

beer
bier

beet
beat

befallen
befell

began
begun

being
bean
been

belief
believe

bell
belle

bellow
below

beret
berry
bury

berth
birth

beside
besides

184

between	boost	breath	cart
among	boast	breathe	kart
bid	bootee	bred	cartilage
bade	booty	bread	cartridge
bier	border	breech	cartridge
beer	boarder	breach	cartilage
bight	bore	bridal	cash
bite	boar	bridle	cache
byte	boor		
birth	born	Britain	cast
berth	borne	Briton	caste
bit		broach	catholic
bitten	borough	brooch	Catholic
bite	burgh	broke	cause
bight	borrow	broken	coarse
byte	lend	brooch	course
bizarre	bough	broach	cavalier
bazaar	bow	buoy	cavalry
blew	boulder	boy	ceiling
blown	bolder	burgh	sealing
blew	bound	borough	cell
blue	bounded	bury	sell
bloc	bouquet	beret	censor
block	bookie	berry	censure
blown	bow	but	cent
blew	beau	butt	scent
blue	bow	buy	sent
blew	bough	by	centenarian
boar	bowled	bye	centenary
boor	bold	byte	charted
bore		bight	chartered
board	boy	bite	chased
bored	buoy	cache	chaste
boarder	brae	cash	cheap
border	bray	callous	cheep
boast	brake	callus	check
boost	break	came	cheque
bold	brassière	come	checked
bowled	brazier	candid	chequered
bolder	bray	candied	cheep
boulder	brae	cannon	cheap
bonny	breach	canon	cheque
bony	breech	can't	check
bookie	bread	cant	choir
bouquet	bred	canvas	quire
boor	break	canvass	choose
boar	brake	carat	chose
bore		carrot	

185

chord
cord

chose
choose
chosen

chute
shoot

cite
sight
site

clothes
cloths

coarse
course
cause

collage
college

colonel
kernel

coma
comma

come
came

comma
coma

commissionaire
commissioner

complement
compliment

complementary
complimentary

concert
consort

confidant
confidante
confident

conscience
conscientious
conscious

consols
consoles

consort
concert

consul
council
counsel

continual
continuous

coop
coup

coral
corral

cord
chord

co-respondent
correspondent

cornet
coronet

cornflour
cornflower

coronet
cornet

corps
corpse

corral
coral

correspondent
co-respondent

cost
costed

could
canned

council
counsel
consul

councillor
counsellor

coup
coop

course
coarse
cause

courtesy
curtsy

crevasse
crevice

cue
queue

curb
kerb

currant
current

curtsy
courtesy

cygnet
signet

cymbal
symbol

dairy
diary

dam
damn

dammed
damned

damn
dam

decry
descry

delusion
allusion
illusion

demean
demesne
domain

dependant
dependent

deprecate
depreciate

descendant
descendent

descent
dissent

descry
decry

desert
dessert

device
devise

devolution
evolution

dew
due
Jew

diary
dairy

did
done

die
dye

died
dyed

disbelief
disbelieve

disburse
disperse

discreet
discrete

discus
discuss

disperse
disburse

dissent
descent

domain
demean
demesne

done
did

draft
draught

draught
draft

drawn
drew

drank
drunk

drew
drawn

driven
drove

drunk
drank

dual
duel

ducks
dux

dudgeon
dungeon

due
dew
Jew

duel
dual

dully
duly

dungeon
dudgeon

dux
ducks

dye
die

dyed
died

dyeing
dying

easterly
eastern

eatable
edible

eclipse
ellipse

economic
economical

edible
eatable

edition
addition

effect
affect

effluent
affluent

elder
eldest

elicit
illicit

eligible
legible

ellipse
eclipse

elude
allude

emend
amend

emigrant
immigrant

emigration
immigration

emission
omission

emphasis
emphasize

employee
employer

ensure
insure

envelop
envelope

epigram
epitaph
epithet

ere
err

erotic
erratic

err
ere

erratic
erotic

essay
assay

evolution
devolution

ewe
yew
you

except
accept

excess
access

executioner
executor

exercise
exorcise

expand
expend

expansive
expensive

expatiate
expiate

expend
expand

expensive
expansive

expiate
expatiate

extant
extinct

fain
feign

faint
feint

fair
fare

fallen
fell
felled

fare
fair

fate
fête

feat
feet

feign
fain

feint
faint

fell
fallen
felled

ferment
foment

fête
fate

fiancé
fiancée

filed
filled

final
finale

fission
fissure

flair
flare

flea
flee

flew
flu
flue

flew
flown

floe
flow

flour
flower

floury
flowery

flow
floe

flower
flour

flowery
floury

flown
flew
flu

flue
flew

foment
ferment

font
fount

forbade
forbidden

fore
four

foregone
forgone

foresaw
foreseen

foreword
forward

forgave
forgiven

forgone
foregone

forgone
forwent

forgot
forgotten

forsaken
forsook

forswore
forsworn

fort
forte

forty
forth
fourth

forty
fort
forte

forward
foreword

forwent
forgone

found
founded

fount
font

four
fore

fourth
forth

franc
frank

funeral
funereal

gabble
gable

gait
gate

galleon
gallon

gamble
gambol

gaol
goal

gate
gait

gave
given

genie
genius
genus

genteel
gentile
gentle

genus
genie
genius

gild
guild

gilt
guilt

given
gave

glacier
glazier

goal
gaol

gone
went

gorilla
guerrilla

gourmand
gourmet

gradation
graduation

grate
great

grew
grown

grief
grieve

grill
grille

griped
gripped

grisly
gristly
grizzly

grope

group

ground
grounded

grown

grew

guerrilla
gorilla

guild
gild

guilt
gilt

hail
hale
hair
hare
half
halve
hallo
hallow
halo
halve
half
hangar
hanger
hanged
hung
hanger
hangar

hare
hair

hart
heart

heal
heel

hear
here

heart
hart

heel
heal

heir
air

here
hear

hid
hidden

higher
hire

him
hymn

hire
higher

hoar
whore

hoard
horde

hole
whole

honorary
honourable

hoped
hopped

horde
hoard

human
humane

humiliation
humility

hung
hanged

hymn
him

idle
idol

illegible
ineligible

illicit
elicit

illiterate
alliterate

illusion
allusion
delusion

immigrant
emigrant

immigration
emigration

immoral
amoral
immortal

immorality
immortality

impetuous
impetus

impracticable
impractical

impressed
imprest

in
inn

inapt
inept

incredible
incredulous

indigenous
indigent

industrial
industrious

ineligible
illegible

inept
inapt

ingenious
ingenuous

inhuman
inhumane

inn
in

insure
ensure

188

intelligent	lade	lightening	mail
intelligible	laid	lightning	male
interment	lay	lineament	main
internment	lied	liniment	mane
invertebrate	lain	liqueur	maize
inveterate	lane	liquor	maze
it's	lair	literal	male
its	layer	literary	mail
jam	lane	literate	mane
jamb	lain	load	main
Jew	laterally	lode	maniac
dew	latterly	loan	manic
due	lath	lone	manner
jib	lathe	loath	manor
jibe	latterly	loathe	mare
judicial	laterally	local	mayor
judicious	lay	locale	marina
junction	lade	lode	merino
juncture	laid	load	
	lied	lone	marshal
kart		loan	martial
cart	layer		martial
kerb	lair	looped	marshal
curb	lead	loped	
	led	lopped	mask
key			masque
quay	leak	loose	mat
	leek	lose	matt
knave	led	loot	mayor
nave	lead	lute	mare
knead	leek	loped	maze
kneed	leak	lopped	maize
need	legible	looped	
knew	eligible	lose	mean
known	lend	loose	mien
knew	borrow	loth	meat
new	lessen	loathe	meet
	lesson		mete out
knight	liable	lumbar	
night	libel	lumber	medal
knightly	liar	lute	meddle
nightly	lyre	loot	mediate
			meditate
knot	libel	lyre	meet
not	liable	liar	meat
knotty	licence	made	mete out
naughty	license	maid	merino
know	lied	magnate	marina
no	lade	magnet	metal
known	laid	maid	mettle
knew	lay	made	

189

mete out
meat
meet

meter
metre

mettle
metal

mews
muse

mien
mean

might
mite

miner
minor

minister
minster

missal
missile

mistaken
mistook

mite
might

moat
mote

modal
model
module

momentary
momentous
momentum

moped
mopped

moral
morale

morality
mortality

mote
moat

motif
motive

mucous
mucus

multiple
multiply

muscle
mussel

muse
mews

mussel
muscle

mystic
mystique

naught
nought

naughty
knotty

naval
navel

nave
knave

navel
naval

navvy
navy

nay
née
neigh

need
knead
kneed

negligent
negligible

neigh
nay
née

net
nett

new
knew

night
knight

nightly
knightly

no
know

northerly
northern

not
knot

nought
naught

oar
ore

of
off

official
officious

omission
emission

oral
aural

ore
oar

organism
orgasm

outdid
outdone

overcame
overcome

overran
overrun

overtaken
overtook

overthrew
overthrown

packed
pact

pail
pale

pain
pane

pair
pare
pear

palate
palette
pallet

pale
pail

palette
palate
pallet

pane
pain

par
parr

pare
pear
pair

parol
parole

parr
par

passed
past

peace
piece

peak
peek
pique

peal
peel

pear
pair
pare

pedal
peddle

peek
peak
pique

peel
peal

peer
pier

pence
pennies

pendant
pendent

pennies
pence

perquisite
prerequisite

personal
personnel

petrel
petrol

piece
peace

pier
peer

pined
pinned

piped
pipped

pique
peak
peek

190

pistil	price	quite	reign
pistol	prise	quiet	rain
place	prize	racket	rein
plaice	principal	racquet	relief
plain	principle	radar	relieve
plane	prise	raider	reproof
plaintiff	price	raged	reprove
plaintive	prize	ragged	respectful
plait	private	raider	respective
plate	privet	radar	rest
plane	prize	rain	wrest
plain	prise	reign	review
plate	price	rein	revue
plait	proceed	raise	ridden
plum	precede	raze	rode
plumb	profit	rampant	right
politic	prophet	rampart	rite
political	program	ran	write
pool	programme	run	ring
pull	proof	rang	wring
poplar	prove	ringed	ringed
popular	property	rung	rang
pore	propriety	rap	rung
pour	prophecy	wrap	risen
pored	prophesy	raped	rose
poured	prophet	rapped	rite
poser	profit	rapped	right
poseur	propriety	rapt	write
pour	property	wrapped	road
pore	prostate	rated	rode
poured	prostrate	ratted	rowed
pored	prove	raze	rode
practicable	proof	raise	ridden
practical	pull	read	roe
practice	pool	red	row
practise	put	read	rôle
pray	putt	reed	roll
prey	quash	real	rose
precede	squash	reel	risen
proceed	quay	red	rote
premier	key	read	wrote
première	queue	reed	rough
prerequisite	cue	read	ruff
perquisite	quiet	reel	rout
prey	quite	real	route
pray	quire	refuge	row
	choir	refugee	roe

rowed
road
rode

ruff
rough

run
ran

rung
wrung

rye
wry

sail
sale

salon
saloon

salvage
selvage

sang
sung

sank
sunk
sunken

saviour
savour

saw
seen

sawed
sawn

scared
scarred

scene
seen

scent
cent
sent

sceptic
septic

scraped
scrapped

sculptor
sculpture

sea
see

sealing
ceiling

seam
seem

sear
seer
sere

secret
secrete

see
sea

seem
seam

seen
saw

seen
scene

seer
sear
sere

sell
cell

selvage
salvage

sensual
sensuous

sent
cent
scent

septic
sceptic

sere
sear
seer

series
serious

sew
so
sow

sewer
sower

sewn
sewed

sewn
sown

shaken
shook

shear
sheer

sheared
sheered

shorn

shelf
shelve

shook
shaken

shoot
chute

shorn
sheared
sheered

showed
shown

shrank
shrunk

sight
cite
site

signet
cygnet

silicon
silicone

sinuous
sinus

site
cite
sight

skies
skis

slated
slatted

sloe
slow

sloped
slopped

slow
sloe

smelled
smelt

sniped
snipped

so
sew
sow

soar
sore

sociable
social

solder
soldier

sole
soul

some
sum

son
sun

soot
suit

sore
soar

soul
sole

southerly
southern

sow
sew
so

sowed
sewn

sower
sewer

sown
sewn

spared
sparred

speciality
specialty

species
specious

sped
speeded

spoke
spoken

sprang
sprung

squash
quash

staid
stayed

stair
stare

stake
steak

stalk
stock

stanch
staunch

192

stare	suite	team	tiled
stair	sweet	teem	tilled
stationary	sum	tear	timber
stationery	some	tare	timbre
statue	summary	tear	time
statute	summery	tier	thyme
staunch	sun	teem	tire
stanch	son	team	tyre
stayed	sundae	temporal	to
staid	Sunday	temporary	too
steak	sunk	tendon	two
stake	sank	tenon	toe
steal	sunken	tenor	tow
steel	surplice	tenure	tomb
step	surplus	testimonial	tome
steppe	sweet	testimony	ton
stile	suite	their	tonne
style	swelled	there	tun
stimulant	swollen	they're	too
stimulus	swingeing	thorough	to
stock	swinging	through	two
stalk	swollen	thrash	took
stocked	swelled	thresh	taken
stoked	swore	threw	topi
storey	sworn	through	toupee
story	symbol	threw	tore
straight	cymbal	thrown	torn
strait	tacks	throes	tow
straightened	tax	throws	toe
straitened	tail	throne	trait
stratum	tale	thrown	tray
stratus	taken	through	treaties
strewed	took	thorough	treatise
strewn	tale	through	trod
strife	tail	threw	trodden
strive	taped	thrown	troop
striped	tapped	threw	troupe
stripped	taper	thrown	tun
strive	tapir	throne	ton
strife	tapped	throws	tonne
striven	taped	throes	turban
strove	tare	thyme	turbine
style	tear	time	two
stile	taught	tied	to
suit	taut	tide	too
soot	tax	tier	tycoon
	tacks	tear	typhoon

tyre
tire

unaware
unawares

unconscionable
unconscious

undid
undone

unwanted
unwonted

urban
urbane

vacation
vocation

vain
vane
vein

vale
veil

venal
venial

veracity
voracity

vertex
vortex

vicious
vitious

vigilant
vigilante

vitious
vicious

vocation
vacation

voracity
veracity

vortex
vertex

wafer
waiver
waver

waged
wagged

waif
waive
wave

waist
waste

waiver
wafer
waver

want
wont

warden
warder

ware
wear

waste
waist

wave
waif
waive

waver
wafer
waiver

way
weigh

weak
week

wear
ware

weekly
weakly

weigh
way

went
gone

westerly
western

wet
whet

whit
wit

whole
hole

whore
hoar

willed
would

winded
wound

wit
whit

withdrawn
withdrew

wittily
wittingly

woe
woo

woke
woken

wont
want

woo
woe

wore
worn

work-in
working

would
willed

would
wood
wooed

wove
woven

wrap
rap

wrapped
rapped
rapt

wreak
wreck

wreath
wreathe

wrest
rest

wretch
retch

wring
ring

write
right
rite

wrote
rote

wrote
written

wrung
rung

wry
rye

yew
ewe
you

yoke
yolk

yore
your

Some commonly used abbreviations

The typist should always check whether abbreviations can be used. As a general rule abbreviations do not appear in formal documents.

In addition, the ampersand sign (&=and) or its handwritten equivalent is often used in drafts, but must *always* be typed in full except in certain special cases. If in doubt, the typist should always expand it, as this is more acceptable than the ampersand used incorrectly.

a/c	account	cd	could
ACAS	Advisory, Conciliation and Arbitration Service	c/f	carried forward (accounts)
ad, advert	advertisement	cf	compare (Latin: *confer*)
ADC	advise duration and charge	cif	cost, insurance, freight
		cm	centimetre
ADP	automatic data processing	Co	Company (except in registered company names)
AGM	Annual General Meeting	c/o	care of
ALGOL	Algorithmic Language (computers)	COBOL	Common Business-Orientated Language (computers)
APR	annual percentage rate	cod	cash on delivery
ans	answer	COI	Central Office of Information
AOB	Any Other Business	cont, contd	continued
approx	approximately	cr	credit (accounts)
Apr	April	Cresc	Crescent
asap	as soon as possible	CV	curriculum vitae
Asst	Assistant	Dec	December
Aug	August	Dept	Department
Ave	Avenue	doz	dozen
BASIC	Beginners' All-Purpose Symbolic Instruction Code (computers)	DP	data processing
		dr	debit (in accounts)
		DSS	Department of Social Security
Benelux	Belgium, Netherlands and Luxembourg	E and OE	errors and omissions excepted
b/f	brought forward (accounts)	ECU	European currency unit
bk	book	EDP	electronic data processing
bldg	building		
bn	billion	EC	European Community
Bros	Brothers (in company names)	EFTA	European Free Trade Association
BSI	British Standards Institution	eg	for example (Latin: *exempli gratia*)
BT	British Telecom	EMF	European Monetary Fund
C	Centigrade, Celsius		
c	about (Latin: *circa*)	EMS	European Monetary System
caps	capitals		
CAT, CT	computer-aided typesetting	EOC	Equal Opportunities Commission
CBI	Confederation of British Industry	esp	especially
		Esq	Esquire

etc	and so on (Latin: *et cetera*)	Ltd	Limited Liability (in company names)
est	established	LV	luncheon voucher
et seq	and the following (Latin: *et sequens*)	Man Dir	Managing Director
		Mar	March
ext	extension	max	maximum
F	Fahrenheit	mfr(s)	manufacturer(s)
fas	free alongside ship	memo	memorandum
Feb	February	MEP	Member of the European Parliament
FIFO	first in, first out		
fob	free on board	Messrs	Sirs (French: *Messieurs*)
for	free on rail		
FORTRAN	Formula Translation	min	minimum, minute
Fri	Friday	ml	millilitre
fwd	forward	MLR	minimum lending rate
g	gram(me)	mm	millimetre
Gdns	Gardens	Mon	Monday
GDP	Gross Domestic Product	MS	manuscript
		MSS	manuscripts
GNP	Gross National Product	NB	take note (Latin: *nota bene*)
Govt	Government		
HMSO	Her Majesty's Stationery Office	nem con	no-one contradicting (Latin: *nemine contradicente*)
Hon Sec	Honorary Secretary		
HP	hire purchase	nem diss	no-one dissenting (Latin: *nemine dissentiente*)
hr	hour		
HSE	Health and Safety Executive		
		no	number
IC	integrated circuit	Nov	November
ie	that is (Latin: *id est*)	nr	near
Inc	Incorporated (in company names)	O & M	Organization and Methods
inc, incl	including, inclusive	OCR	optical character recognition
inv	invoice		
IOU	I owe you	Oct	October
ISBN	International Standard Book Number	OFT	Office of Fair Trading
		OHMS	On Her Majesty's Service
IT	Information Technology		
Jan	January	OPEC	Organization of Petroleum Exporting Countries
JP	Justice of the Peace		
Jul	July		
Jun	June	oz	ounce
lc	lower case	PA	Personal Assistant
K	kilo=thousand (especially in compounds)	pa	per annum
		PA(B)X	Private Automatic (Branch) Exchange
kg	kilogram(me)	p & p	postage and packing
km	kilometre	PAYE	Pay As You Earn
kW	kilowatt	PC	personal computer
LCD	liquid crystal display	PCB	printed circuit board
LED	light-emitting diode	PLC	Public Limited Company (in company names)
lh	left-hand		
LIFO	last in, first out		
LILO	last in, last out	po	postal order

pp	for and on behalf of (Latin: *per procurationem*)	tel	telephone
		temp	temporary
		Thur	Thursday
pp	pages	TUC	Trades Union Congress
PR	Public Relations		
PROM	programmable read-only memory	Tues	Tuesday
		uc	upper case
QC	Queen's Counsel	UHF	ultra-high frequency
qv	which see (Latin: *quod vide*)	UV	ultra-violet
		VAT	Value Added Tax
RAM	random-access memory	VCR	video cassette recorder
		VDU	visual display unit
R & D	research and development	VHF	very high frequency
		viz	namely (Latin: *videlicet*)
R/D	refer to drawer	vol	volume
Rd	Road	VTR	video tape recorder
re	with reference to	wd	would
recd	received	Wed	Wednesday
ref	reference	wef	with effect from
rep	representative	wk	week
rh	right-hand	WP	word processing
ROM	read-only memory	wpm	words per minute
RPI	Retail Price Index	Xmas	Christmas
sae	stamped, addressed envelope	yr	year, your
		@	at (accounts)
Sat	Saturday	©	copyright
SAYE	Save As You Earn	¢	cent
sec	second	°	degrees
Sept	September	£	pounds
shd	should	#	number
Sq	Square	%	per cent
St	Street	®	registered trademark
STD	Subscriber Trunk Dialling	$	dollars
		¥	yen

Principal Cities and Countries of the World

This is not intended to be a comprehensive list, but merely a reference list for the typist of most of the place names likely to be encountered in a business office. It should be noted that the spellings used here are, in all cases, those used in English-speaking countries. Local spelling variations of some place names exist, and it is advisable to use these when addressing envelopes for the post. Reference to a good atlas will give the localized spelling where appropriate.

Aberdeen
Adelaide
Algeria
Amsterdam
Ankara
Argentina
Athens
Auckland
Australia
Austria

Baghdad
Barcelona
Beijing
  (formerly Peking)
Beirut
Belfast
Belgium
Belgrade
Berlin
Berne
Birmingham
Bombay
Bonn
Boston
Brazil
Brisbane
Brussels
Bucharest
Budapest
Buenos Aires

Cairo
Calcutta
Canada
Canberra
Chicago
Chile
China
Cologne
Colombo
Copenhagen
Cracow
Czechoslovakia

Delhi
Denmark
Detroit
Dublin
Durban
Düsseldorf

Edinburgh
Egypt
Eire

Finland
Florence
France
Frankfurt

Geneva
Genoa
Germany
Glasgow
Greece

Hamburg
Hanover
Harare
Helsinki
Hong Kong
Hungary

Iceland
India
Iran
Iraq
Israel
Istanbul
Italy

Japan
Johannesburg
Jordan

Karachi
Kenya
Kiev
Korea

Kowloon
Kuwait

Lagos
Lebanon
Leeds
Leicester
Leningrad
Lisbon
Liverpool
London
Los Angeles
Lusaka
Luxembourg
Lyons

Madrid
Manchester
Marseilles
Melbourne
Middlesbrough
Milan
Montreal
Moscow
Munich

Nairobi
Naples
Netherlands
New York
New Zealand
Nigeria
Norway

Osaka
Oslo
Ottawa

Pakistan
Paris
Peking
  (now Beijing)
Philadelphia
Poland

Portugal
Prague

Qatar
Quebec

Reykjavik
Rio de Janeiro
Romania/Rumania
Rome
Rotterdam

San Francisco
Santiago
Saudi Arabia
Seoul

Spain
Sri Lanka
Stockholm
Stuttgart
Sweden
Switzerland
Sydney

Taiwan
Teheran
Thailand
The Hague
Tokyo
Toronto
Turin
Turkey

Vancouver
Venice
Vienna

Warsaw
Washington
Wellington
Winnipeg

Yugoslavia

Zambia
Zimbabwe
Zürich